Inquire about speaking or consulting at: schewiorb@gmail.com

Or visit his website at DeconstructingTennis.com

ISBN – 13: 978-0692865156 (Tennis Development Press)

ISBN – 10: 0692865152

Published in the USA by Tennis Development Press

Katonah, NY 10536

Printed by GFI Communications Corp

Peekskill, NY

Cover designed by Sara Pena

Table of Contents

Foreword

I met "Schev" when I was a graduate student in English literature at Rutgers University; he was the number one singles player on the Rutgers tennis team. I practiced with team players indoors in the winter, outdoors in warm weather. The Rutgers tennis team played against other college teams, including Columbia University, where Vitas Gerulaitis was a young player, just prior to his professional career. Since 1975, Schewior has been the Director of Tennis at Chestnut Ridge Racquet Club in Mt. Kisco, NY. His long-awaited book is a distillation of four decades of daily observation and learning, offering keen contextual understanding—for players seeking to play with confidence and purpose. Schewior cites the methods and thinking of a broad range of contemporary coaches, organizing their insights in ways that offer fresh understandings, which deepen our sheer pleasure in playing. Few tennis coaches offer more penetrating comprehension into the exciting dynamics of how pivotal moments in a match often hinge upon subtle adjustments in shot selection, pace of shot, tension control, and observational neutrality.

In his 1938 book, Homo Ludens, Johan Huizinga delineates the five key elements of play. Schewior hones in on Huizinga's #1 idea: Play is freedom. He has also conveyed in private conversation with me:"Competence creates joy. Once a player is competent, she is free." His 4-D System does not only make you a better tennis player; it provides you with both a framework for personal exploration and a path to personal acceptance.

Schewior's motivation to teach was simply that it afforded him a way to work on his own game. He told me: "I took every opportunity to focus and run down every ball. I distinctly remember an eight-hour teaching day during which not one ball bounced twice on my side of the net. Relative to my peers, I kept improving until injuries forced me out of top-level competition. This was proof to me that the insights gained from my own competitive experiences were valuable." There is an element of spontaneity in live play that no calculation can foresee. Here Robert Schewior's astute contextual analysis of the inner drama of tennis is calmly dissected and then reassembled into a coherent whole by a seasoned coach who is also a trained economist. Economics, often depicted as a "dismal science," which forces trade-offs between guns and butter, is also fundamentally a calculus of choice. Schewior teaches us how to make informed and intelligent decisions through both general discussions of topics like Percentage Tennis and simple illustrative examples to make his points. He has a unique ability to both simplify and explain key concepts and to reinforce these concepts with entertaining anecdotal evidence.

Schewior's 4-D System provides a framework for creating a safe space. As you become accomplished at implementing it, pressure situations won't impress themselves as they once used to. You become free to play with a spontaneous mindfulness. This book will become a classic.

CHRISTOPHER BUSA was the Head Tennis Professional at the Provincetown Tennis Club from 1970-1984 and was a member of the USPTA. He is currently the founder and editorial director of Provincetown Arts Press.

Introduction

Tennis has been around as a sport since the late 1860's and most of the Rules of the Game have not changed. For example, the dimensions of the court and the height of the net have remained the same. Beginning in 1961, it was no longer required to have one foot on the ground when making contact with a serve. Otherwise, the tennis of the 1860's is the tennis of today.

In addition, the scoring system has remained largely the same. The introduction of the tiebreak in 1970 added both increased point importance, and therefore, drama, at the end of a set. This is a minor tweak.

However, the technological improvements with respect to both the racquets and the strings have changed tennis in a major way. These improvements have made possible certain shots which were literally impossible to make when tennis was in its wooden racquet phase. The modern game requires a Herculean combination of strength, speed, and endurance along with a mastery of shot selection and tactics.

Has the mental game in tennis also evolved? Has there been a concomitant rise in the mental strength, flexibility, and consistency of tennis players? A day at the US Open tells us all we need to know. The shrieks of frustration, the smashed racquets, and a host of other unconstructive responses all point to the fact that the minds of most players are still far away from where they would like to be. A similar story can be told for club players at all levels.

My claim is that there is a 4-step mental process (the 4-D System!) which can be implemented between points to give any player a far better chance of accessing their best tennis. Implementing this System without wavering is equivalent to switching from a wooden to a modern racquet. Deconstructing Tennis will offer you a major upgrade in your mental approach to the game.

Chapter 1

Why Deconstructing Tennis?

To "deconstruct" means to get to what's essential. This book will share with you the essentials of exactly what the top pros do with their mental game that can be replicated by you. Any player, from a solid club-level player to a member of the professional tour, can improve by implementing the mental system explained in this book.

By most estimates, the ball is not in play about 80% of the time during a competitive match. Knowing how to use this time effectively is one of the keys to success in tennis. My basic claim is that any player willing to program/reprogram his mental processes during this time will experience dramatically higher levels of success. A mere 2% improvement in the number of points won against an evenly matched opponent improves a player's odds of winning a match from 50% to just over 70% (see Chapter 5)! This improvement can come from a variety of sources: better shot selection, improved tension control, or better ball-watching skills. The 4-D System will give you the ability to improve in ALL of these areas. This suggests that reaching the 2% improvement mark should not be difficult if you are prepared to put in the time to learn the 4-D System. 4-D is shorthand for the mental processes which should be put into place between each point, as well as on the changeovers.

Every decent tennis player understands the importance of recovering back to the proper court position after a shot has been hit. Without this recovery, a player could not hope to defend her court. Analogously, there is a "mental recovery" which goes on between the finish of one point until the start of the next. This recovery allows a player to understand and accept what has just happened, while also preparing for the point to come. Yet far too many players ignore this crucial recovery to the detriment of their ability to build confidence when things are going in their favor or to halt an opponent's run of points when things are going poorly. As match pressure increases, players tend to do less and less well with their mental recovery. This is simply because pressure changes the way that we react. However, if you have repeatedly practiced the step-by-step processes which comprise the 4-D System, you will be far better at maintaining your level of play at the decisive moments of a match.

The mental component of tennis has been hinted at and been given significant credit for separating winners from losers in the professional ranks by former top players who commentate on televised matches, but never given the in-depth look that this book will provide.

In their book, Analyzing Wimbledon: The Power of Statistics (2014), Franc Klaasen and Jan Magnus demonstrate with real-world data from professional tennis that the mental component separates the better from the weaker players. They write:

Players are trained by their coaches to be mentally stable, forget about the score, forget about the past, and focus on the current point ... Top players do not perform better, but lower-ranked players perform worse, at important points.[1]

The mental component which separates winners from losers requires an unwavering discipline which demands that you ALWAYS play from within the system. It is this discipline which allows the top players to handle the pressures of competitive tennis most of the time.

At the same time, it's important to acknowledge that, while the mental game is an important component in any player's arsenal, it is NOT the entire game of tennis. Players still need to work on developing better technique and better conditioning. Witness the success of Novak Djokovic in 2011. His service technique improved, he gained speed and endurance, but he also became significantly better at managing his emotions and his focus. One has only to look at his reactions and composure between points to see that this was a big part of his success.

[1] Analyzing Wimbledon, p.173ff.

The 4-Dimensional System (4-D System)

1) Observe What Happened
2) Adjust/Plan
3) Manage Tension
4) Watch the Ball

Deconstructing Tennis will provide you with a blueprint of the step-by-step process by which top players stay mentally tough through both the good times and the bad. (I mention the "good times" because even top players have blown leads.) In this respect, this book is different from every other book on mental toughness that has previously been written. It is the systematic approach to a between-points regimen which separates this book from all other mental training approaches.

For example, in his work, Jim Loehr, a mental training guru, provides a checklist of qualities and reactions which he would like to instill in his athletes. Each of them is admirable. In Chapter 15 of The New Toughness Training For Sports he lists 17 strategies for mental toughness. In particular, LEARN TO KEEP A HERE-AND-NOW FOCUS DURING COMPETITION gives strong support to the development of something like the 4-D System. 4-D teaches you the what and when which you should pay attention to in the here-and-now.

In addition, Dr. Loehr has popularized "The 16-Second Cure", his approach to using the time between points[2]. The 16 seconds refers to the approximate time that players have between points and his suggestion that this time be used for emotional stability and control again gives credence to the idea that the time between points is critical for all players.

Allen Fox has also contributed meaningfully to the discussion of the mental side of tennis. His book, Tennis: Winning the Mental Match, contains many useful and insightful tips and suggestions. Insights like "Slow down when you are

[2] Mental Toughness Training for Tennis: Volume 1. The 16-Second Cure, Youtube, Nov. 24, 2015, 28:03.

behind" and "Never show weakness" are very valuable. However, Deconstructing Tennis is different from both of these approaches in that it puts the mental components of your between-point ritual into a clear four-step process (4D!).

Deconstructing Tennis also goes beyond the 4-D System to make diverse subjects such as shot selection, point importance, and the ideal framing of one's expectations resonate for all of you. These discussions serve to reveal the strategic foundations of tennis and demonstrate clearly how tennis is, in fact, a lot like chess. In other words, good decision-making in tennis has a rational basis.

I also include key findings from behavioral psychology. In particular, I will show you how to "frame" a match so that you may adjust your expectations in a way that will free you to play your better tennis.

Significant findings from sports psychology are also presented with an analysis of the optimal level of risk to be taken at different moments in a match, so that you will have a reason for "going for it." In addition, Sports Psychology tells us that there is an optimal level of tension under which we all play at our best. Most often, match pressure carries us to a place where we are trying too hard. The 4-D System will make you a far better manager of both your physical and emotional tension levels.

In effect, the 4-D System brings about the marriage of rationality, psychology, and Zen.

As a player, you must be able to formulate a game plan based upon both an understanding of "Percentage Tennis" and the matchups that exist between your own and your opponent's strengths and weaknesses. This is the key to defeating players who are "better." You need to be able to construct points so that your best shot is matching up with your opponent's weakest shot as often as possible. Chapter 4 will explain Percentage Tennis and Court Geometry. Once you grasp these concepts, it will be possible to integrate them into your game plan and then into the 4-D System.

The words "percentage" and "geometry" hint that playing better tennis is connected to math skills. This has been corroborated by a study which showed better college players to have relatively higher math SAT scores. Before any of you elects to abandon this book because you hate math or see yourself as a math underachiever, rest assured that these concepts are no more sophisticated than middle school math. You can all grasp these concepts with little difficulty.

Secondly, not all points in tennis have an equal influence on the outcome of a match. I will discuss this in more detail, also in Chapter 4, but I think that anyone can see that the value of the 0-0, 0-40 point is not the same as the 5-all, deuce point. This understanding has important implications for exactly when you may choose to play lower percentage shots to keep an opponent honest, as opposed to playing your best percentage shot. By definition, lower percentage shots are more risky. Another way to talk about understanding the scoring system of tennis is simply to say that this understanding will help you to recognize when to take more chances and when to play more solidly (high percentage shots). Understanding the score will make it much easier to decide when to take more risks. Seen in this light, taking more or less risk has a rational basis and is not random.

Thirdly, you must be able to repeatedly hit your targets. A baseball player who hits 3 out of 10 is likely to be in the Hall of Fame; a tennis player who does the same probably won't have any hitting partners. Aside from the repetition which is essential to controlling the ball, the developing of FEEL is essential to mastering ball control. A detailed explanation of FEEL and how to develop it is presented in Chapter 6. FEEL is the foundation upon which the 4-D System rests. No matter how well you may understand what is happening on the court, without the ability to execute your shots, this understanding is close to worthless.

Finally, you will need to learn how to implement the 4-D System during the time between points. A brief overview of 4-D tennis is in Chapter 2 with the subsequent chapters going into more detail and providing concrete examples of the system. This will allow you to integrate your ability to hit targets with an effective game plan while simultaneously accounting for the score and managing your emotional and physical tension levels.

Each of the key concepts to be discussed in Deconstructing Tennis: The 4-D System is approached with a generalized discussion, supplemented by specific examples of certain game situations or players with certain characteristics. In addition, these examples are further supplemented with "stories" from matches at both the professional and club levels.

Specific examples: will be boxed in red and illustrate how to make the implementation of the 4-D System concrete. These illustrations will serve as examples of different aspects of 4-D. At the same time, your ability to grasp the 4-D System as a whole means that these examples represent only a smattering of the range of solutions to the puzzles which you will face as a tennis player. Once you understand how to implement the system, it will enable you consistently to bring your best game to your matches because you will be able to deal with nearly all possible riddles that an opponent poses. Eliminating most of your poorer performances makes you a better player. You can visualize this improvement by thinking of the standard bell curve as describing your current performance levels. If the bottom third of your performances are eliminated, your average performance level will increase.

Stories from professional matches, my own playing career, or club-level matches serve further to clarify the different components of the 4-D System and other concepts such as The Forced Error. These stories will be boxed in blue.

Managing with the 4-D System is all well and good, but you need to know exactly *what* it is that you are managing and *when* you are managing it. Each of the Chapters 3-6 will explain a component of the 4-D System in considerable detail. A mastery of this detail is essential to give you a better chance at success.

For example, a player should engage in tension or arousal management before the start of each point, but major tactical changes are reserved for the changeovers or at the end of a set.

"I submit that tennis is the most beautiful sport there is, and also the most demanding. It requires body control, hand-eye coordination, quickness, flat-out speed, endurance, and that strange mix of caution and abandon we call courage.... No CPU yet existent could compute the expansion of variables for even a single exchange – smoke would come out of the mainframe. The sort of thinking involved is the sort that can be done only by a living and conscious entity, and then only unconsciously, i.e. by combining talent with repetition to such an extent that the variables are combined and controlled without conscious thought. In other words, serious tennis is a kind of art."[3] – David Foster Wallace

Chapter 2

The Four-Dimensional System (4-D)

As I noted in Chapter 1, there are several parts to having a strong mental game. These parts are: playing with FEEL, having a game plan, understanding tennis scoring and risk management, and controlling one's emotions – it all sounds like too much to ask to stay effectively in touch with each of these components of good tennis under the stressful conditions of a match. However, I will show you how to integrate each of these elements in an ordered sequence to digest both what just happened (the previous point) and to prepare for the next point. Again, the four steps of the 4-D System are:

1) Observe What Happened

2) Adjust/Plan

3) Calm Down

4) Watch the Ball

---

[3] Excerpted from David Foster Wallace, 'Tennis Player Michael Joyce's Professional Artistry as a Paradigm of Certain Stuff about Choice, Freedom, Limitation, Joy, Grotesquerie, and Human Completeness', in A Supposedly Fun Thing I'll Never Do Again, 1997, p. 235-236.

Observe What Happened

You must train yourself at the conclusion of each point, to notice immediately what just happened. The length of the point (number of strokes) and the pattern of play which led to the point-ending shot must be observed and filed for reference. Top players update this information after every point. Usually, this means noticing if the point ended on a winner or an error by either you or your opponent. It is also at this time that you begin to "Build an Inventory" of your opponent's favorite shots. Nearly all players do their favorite things at the start of a match, so each point gives you more and more information about your opponent's tendencies and abilities.

Adjust/Plan

The point-ending shot should then be compared with both your percentage tennis and game- plan frameworks to evaluate the plan's success and then keep or adjust your plan for the next point. You need to ask yourself if you played solid percentage tennis (or not!) and if you stuck to your plan (or not!). A simple plan which has you choosing both a target and a level of risk (racquet speed) is then made for the next point. At this moment, a short "check in" with the score may have you changing the appropriate level of risk for the upcoming point. At extremes in the score, 40-0 or 0-40 for example, the plan may deviate from percentage tennis to a higher-risk alternative.

Calm Down

There are two components to calming down. The calming should happen on both the physical level – you will execute your shots better if your body is relaxed, and on the emotional level - you will make better decisions if you are not playing from a place of frustration, anger, stress, or fear.

Watch the Ball

Once you have gone through the first three steps it is crucial to remind yourself to see the ball into the strings. This is the key to delivering the ball to its intended target. The best laid plans will come to naught, if you do not implement the ability to watch the ball once the point begins. In their book Tennis Science (2015), Reid, Elliott, and Crespo call this "gaze behavior" and note that the top players play with "total fixation", Federer-like, so their heads remain still until a stroke is completed.

I will now take you through the four steps of the 4-D System in more detail. Here you will see more of what is involved at each step as well as get specific examples of *how* to use your mind between points.

Chapter 3

Observe What Happened (1) – in detail

Observing What Happened (1) is your ability to “see” what happened during the point that was just completed. I have placed “seeing” in quotation marks because sometimes this skill is quite literal – for example, I missed an easy backhand, while at other times it requires you to look at *how* the story of the point unfolded. In other words, “seeing” involves not only strokes, but also the patterns of play.

Very simply, points are fit into a grid based upon whether or not they are won or lost and whether or not the result was a product of luck or skill. As players improve in level, more and more points are decided by skill. Patterns to be REPEATED will be highlighted in green; those to be AVOIDED in red.

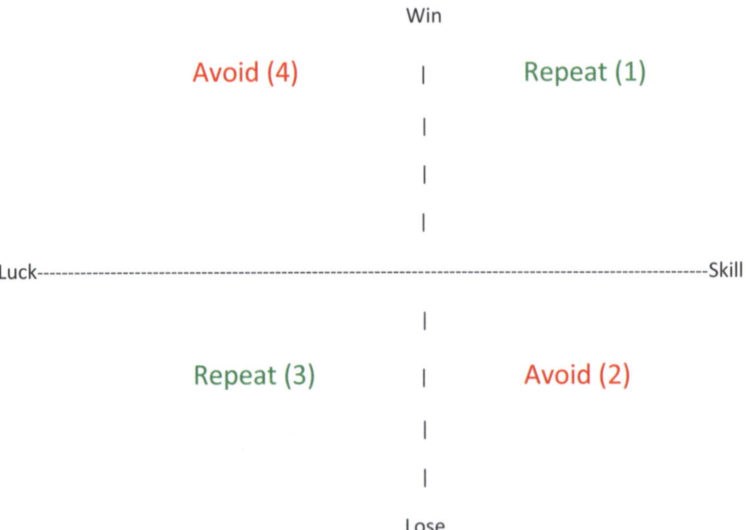

If you should win a point with a particular pattern of play and if this pattern is repeatable, you should notice how the point was won and look to REPEAT (1) the pattern. Whether or not the pattern should be repeated immediately or at some later stage of the match will be discussed later. Suffice it to say, it's important to "see" how a point is won or lost.

To be sure, top players are not actually asking a question like: where does this point fit on my Win/Lose Luck/Skill grid? However, they are acting and making decisions *as if* this were the case. When first learning the 4-D System, you need explicitly to ask yourself this question until such time as it becomes internalized and happens without thought.

Here are a couple of examples from REPEAT (1), the Win/Skill quadrant:

A player serves a wide slice serve to the deuce court and elicits a short return which leads to winning the point with an approach shot. This serve should be REPEATED later in the match.

Or, in a singles match where both players are consistently getting the ball deep and there is not much to separate the players, one of them inadvertently mishits a ball short and notices that her opponent struggles to do anything with this ball. She immediately begins to use purposeful short slices to get her opponent out of her comfort zone (the backcourt) and turns a close match into a one-sided victory.

Conversely, if a player serves the wide slice in the deuce court and watches a forehand bullet scream down the line for a winner, this is a pattern which should be AVOIDED (2). It fits into the Lose/Skill quadrant, particularly if it happens more than twice.

In the last example above, you would like to react to the bullet return of serve winner with a question: If my serve had been better placed, would it have caused trouble for my opponent? This means that you will not make a snap judgment until you have seen at least one more of these returns. If this pattern should occur one or two more times, then you can confidently label it AVOID.

Many modern players like to get to the "dictator position" in baseline rallies. This is when their home base (the position from which they react to an opponent's shot) allows them frequently to run around their backhands. I AVOID this pattern by playing my backhand immediately down the line thereby not allowing my opponent to hit repeated shots from the "dictator position."

You must be able to distinguish between luck and skill on the part of your opponents. If you approach the net behind a high-quality shot only to watch a mishit topspin lob land both over your head and one inch inside the baseline, you should choose to REPEAT (3) this pattern - Lose/Luck.

And finally, if a player attempts to hit the feet of an on-rushing serve-and-volleyer and mistakenly hits a high floater right to her only to have her frame the ball into the back fence, the player would want to AVOID this pattern despite the fact that she won this point - Win/Luck (4). The player would want to test the opponent's volley again at some stage of the match, but probably not with such an easy shot.

As you become better as a player, nearly all of the points are finishing in (1) or (2). This means that you possess the technical ability to change patterns and hit targets. Doing a better job of REPEATING and AVOIDING can often be the difference between winning and losing a match.

Towards the end of my own competitive career, I was greeted at the net at the conclusion of my matches with comments like these: "I hope that I never play you again." "Good win, but I have to say that I played the worst that I have in a long time." "Nice match, I never felt that I got going today." This was all because of my ability to stick relentlessly to the winning patterns which I saw – no exceptions.

To help you to develop your ability to "see" what is happening on the court, you need to use the idea of "The Snapshot." You should take a picture of the court positions of each of the players immediately after the point is concluded. Particularly in doubles, where the patterns are more complex than singles, this will help you to make the subtle adjustments in shot selection or court positioning that will influence the outcome of a match.

If an opponent makes a winning volley from very close to the net, you must be able to adjust so that you don't allow her into that position again. Or, if your partner is caught repeatedly volleying in no-man's land, you need to be able to tell her to establish better attacking- net position.

"Seeing" what just happened within a point and then being able to place it in the appropriate REPEAT/AVOID quadrant is extremely important, but it is also a skill of some subtlety. Sometimes, it is not the point-ending shot which tells the true story – it is a shot played earlier in the point.

For example, when some of my students approach the net and miss a fairly difficult volley, many times they will ask me: what did I do wrong with my volley? Often, the answer is "nothing." The problem was caused by the previous shot, the approach shot in this case, being hit either too short or without sufficient pace. The correct response here is to REPEAT but with the correct gear and placement for the approach shot. If you blame your volley in this example, you will not make any progress with respect to the challenge of changing a losing game into a winning game. On the other hand, the difficult volley could have been caused by the tactical error of approaching to the opponent's stronger side. Here a player would AVOID this wing, but REPEAT the approach to the weaker side when given a similar short ball.

With the advent of the Smartphone, there are many apps which allow a friend/parent to chart your match. These apps all record the final shot of a point as the key datum in making an assessment of your performance. However, poor choices or mediocre execution can be the true cause of unsuccessful plays. These apps do nothing to help you to "see" and to the extent that they purport to explain, they may, in fact, only obscure what is going on. This is not to say that charting a match cannot have some value. On the other hand, it may prevent you from "seeing."

A fairly good 11-year-old failed to attack numerous short forehands with an aggressive approach shot only to lose many points with a missed backhand later in the rally. His dad's app blamed his backhand. What would you say?

The answer to the question of when to REPEAT a Win/Skill pattern can be summarized as follows: if the play that you are running is based upon surprise (like an occasional wide serve to an opponent's forehand in the deuce court), it should be held in reserve (rather like a trump card in bridge) for some future moment. However, if the play is more of a high percentage tennis choice, such as serving down the T to the backhand, it should be repeated immediately so that your opponent begins to develop the sense that she is being controlled. The element of surprise does not matter here. The opponent is fairly certain what is coming, but she can't really do much about it.

Marc Lopez, who is the occasional doubles partner of Rafael Nadal, has a potent forehand and an average backhand. The top pros control him by serving 90% ¾-speed first serves to his backhand. He knows that it's coming, but he can't do much to stop it.

The Snapshot

Implementing your reactions to your observations begins with The Snapshot. At its most basic, The Snapshot means that you must take a picture of both your court position and your opponent's court position along with the shot which was last struck at the moment when the point ends. Mastering The Snapshot allows you to make adjustments in the middle of a match without a large amount of analysis or thinking. This is important because too much thinking will make it very difficult to quiet your mind in preparation for the "Watch the Ball" mode which is necessary for shot execution. In addition, there is not a lot of time between points, so any assessment must be efficient, i.e., done virtually instantaneously.

Rather than step-by-step thought, your reactions will become as simple as: when I see picture X, I respond with shot or movement Y.

In The Snapshot below, Player #4 has approached the net to join her partner. Player #1 drives the ball at Player #3 who plays a winning volley because he is on top of the net. Both of the players on Team Blue must notice this fact and either lob Player #3 or drive the ball to the feet of Player #4 who is further from the net. I would adjust by telling myself the following: next time my opponents are in a similar net position, lob Player #3. When that situation recurs, I do NOT have to think about lobbing. I am only watching the ball into the racquet and letting the programming from The Snapshot control my shot selection.

As players get better at reading various game situations, they become better able to take snapshots while the ball is in play. A snapshot synthesizes court position information with the relevant additional information (your opponent's speed, power and consistency and how these factors match up with your own).

Choosing a good target then simply answers the question: what do I do when I see Snapshot X? As you develop this skill, you will become able to see nuanced differences in snapshots which have previously been indistinguishable. This expansion of your "photo album" will allow you to see, for example, when to close the net against one type of defender and hang back a bit to protect against the lob against another type of defender.

When I hit my first penetrating forehand into my opponent's backhand, I typically charge the net. Against a fast opponent who can move into good position, this first penetrating shot is no longer good enough to follow to the net. The Snapshot tells me to string a few good shots together before I decide to move in.

The Snapshot

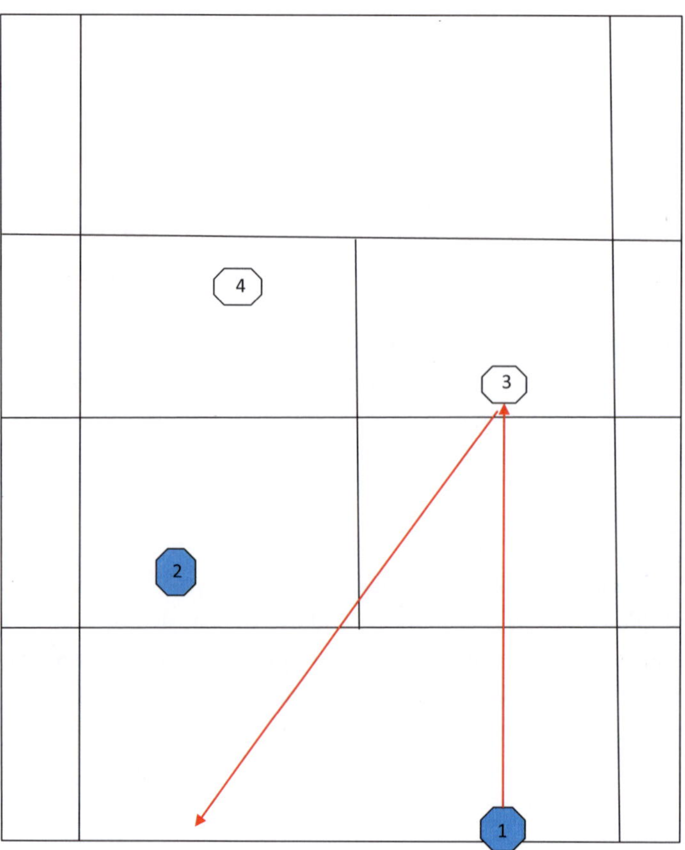

If you have hit your best shot against a player of your level and it comes back for a winner, most likely your opponent was guessing correctly. Since no player can be in all places at all times, The Snapshot will allow you to see which shot you need to use the next time that the same situation comes up.

> ***Roger Federer closes the net and cuts off Andy Murray's perfectly angled passing shot for a winner. Murray will most likely go to the topspin lob the next time Federer comes in.***

It is also at this first stage of the 4-D System that "Building an Inventory" of your opponent's tendencies begins. This is crucial for knowing what you need to do during tight situations such as the end of a set or a tiebreak.

> ***In a 4.0 singles practice session, the favored player was controlling the underdog. Each of the first three times when she got a short backhand, she hit it down the line for a winner. On the fourth such ball, the underdog had not yet anticipated the shot. This means that she was not checking into step (1) of the 4-D system: Observe What Happened and Build An Inventory.***

Building an Inventory

Once the match begins, you should immediately "Build an Inventory" of your opponent's shots. Typically, your opponent will begin a match by doing her favorite things. After a few games, you should be able to answer questions like the following:

Where does she play the ball when I play deep and high?

Where does she play the ball when she gets an approach shot? Does she follow it to the net or hang back?

Does she attack my second serve or merely get it back in play?

Does she prefer to lob or pass when I come up to the net?

Am I winning the shorter points or the longer points?

Once you have started to come up with answers to these questions, and other questions very similar to these, you will be able to anticipate better. Better anticipation means better positioning and therefore a better chance for you to place the ball where you would like.

When you recover to the proper spot at the baseline, small adjustments to your "home base" should be made depending upon what you learn about your opponent. It's just like in doubles where you face an opponent who lobs the return repeatedly – you position yourself a step or two further back from the net as the server's partner. For example, in a recent 4.5 women's singles match, I watched the players exchanging high quality backhands cross court until Player A was able to stretch out Player B with an extra wide backhand and force an error. While this was happening, Player A twice tried to hit her backhand up the line, but was unable to find her target – the ball ended up near the center of the court. Inventory Building would allow Player B to adjust by not recovering all of the way after hitting a cross- court backhand.

By the time you reach the end of the first set or, certainly by the tiebreak, you should have enough information to help you to choose the winning patterns of play. Without the ability to "Build an Inventory" however, each point remains an island unto itself and it will be impossible for you to make the correct adjustments/plans.

Players rarely employ more than two types of return of service on either wing. By the time a tiebreak is reached any opponent is therefore more predictable and you have seen the patterns which win more often. The 4-D System trains players to keep an informal catalog or inventory of an opponent's shots. This catalog is invaluable as you play deeper into a match.

How you choose to react at the start of the match to an opponent's good shots is very important. As you have already seen above, strong shots which can be judged to be a result of skill should be AVOIDED by changing the pattern of play. However, other lower percentage shots should simply be evaluated by judging that pattern with CAUTION. Essentially this means that you suspend judgment pending further information (playing more points). This guarantees that you are not over-reacting to an opponent's good play until you have more time to judge it.

In doubles, my opponent hits a bullet down- the- line return past me at the net. My partner had hit a fairly good first serve. I take note of this shot, but I do not change my game because of it.

Most of this chapter has dealt with recognizing winning/losing patterns of play. However, it is also important to recognize execution errors where either a lack of ball watching, excessive tension levels, or poor footwork can result in lost points. These errors are more easily "seen" and corrected than the shot selection or pattern play errors discussed above.

For example, I might have set up a winning sitter volley only to have the open court distract me from looking the ball into the strings. Or, I might have missed a forehand approach shot because I was trying too hard. These types of errors are noticed and corrected in the Observe What Happened phase of the 4-D System.

Once you are "seeing" what is happening, how do you use this information to plan or adjust for the next point?

"It is easy to be committed to an idea. It is hard to stay committed to a process … Examine yourself without ego. How much wisdom do you really have?" [4] -Sun Tzu

Chapter 4

Formulating a Game Plan – The Foundation of Plan/Adjust (2)

Playing a match is like going to war – the key difference is that victory is symbolic and doesn't result in anyone dying (thank goodness!). There are several components of a well-designed game plan. The goal of this chapter is to illuminate each of these components so that you begin to play with more and more "wisdom."

However, Sun Tzu, in the quotation above, makes it clear that being a great general requires that you remain committed to the process. For our purposes, this simply means that you need to play within the 4-D System. Wisdom, in the quotation above, is linked to process and the contrast between an idea and a process is meant to highlight the mental dexterity that is required to formulate and execute a winning game plan. Ideas tend to be fixed while training yourself to stick to the correct process between points will allow you to make the (often small) adjustments which are necessary to win.

So, being a great general consists of two components: 1) sticking to the process; and 2) formulating a game plan. I will now go into more detail on this second component.

Strategy and tactics can change the outcome of a match between two otherwise equally-matched opponents. In some cases, an excellent game plan can actually propel a weaker player to victory over a player who appears stronger on the surface. Strategy is the overall game plan. Tactics refer to the specific means of implementing any chosen strategy.

For example, my "default game plan" is to pressure an opponent's backhand. This works in most matches. However,

[4] The Art of War, by Sun Tzu,

exceptions do arise and I am always prepared to change. Pressuring my opponent's backhand is therefore my "default" strategy. A possible tactic would be to serve and volley against his backhand in order to place immediate stress on his weakness.

Noah Rubin, ranked #328 at the start of the 2016 Australian Open defeated #17 Benoir Paire in the first round. This was a major upset. He commented: "He's an extremely talented individual. He can come up with drop shots, hasn't missed a backhand in six years, so I kind of knew my game plan (hitting to his forehand), and I stuck to it pretty well."

As you will see, there are certain Immutable Laws of Tennis which cannot be altered. If you think that you have your own "strategies", which work for you and you alone, you really need to read this chapter until its contents is fully internalized. There are no exceptions to some of the laws of tennis which I will cover. If you think that you are the exception and you can consistently violate these laws, you will almost certainly relegate yourself to coming in second in a two-horse race.

Years ago, a fairly high level male player came to me for a lesson. I asked him what he would like to work on and he said: "I have a weakness. When I'm 10 feet behind the baseline, I cannot hit a winner with my backhand." He didn't take my word for it that this could not be taught and, to this day, he continues to come in second. As you will see below, he is a player who thinks he can rewrite the principles of Court Geometry.

Designing a game plan becomes easier with practice, so if you are relatively new to this part of tennis, you should practice this skill when playing in your "fun" games. This will improve your ability to carry it over into competitive situations. A well-designed game plan is, nearly always, a simple plan.

The Immutable Laws of Tennis

Percentage Tennis

This is an often cited term which is sometimes misunderstood. Percentage Tennis involves selecting a shot at any moment in a point that leads to the highest probability of winning that point from that moment forward given the court position of both players, the difficulty of the shot being hit, and the ability levels of the two players.

Percentage Tennis does **not** mean choosing the shot that will go in the highest percentage of the time. If it did, it would mean that percentage tennis would be epitomized by the "grinders" or "pushers" who slow down every game with their bloops and lobs and the smartest players, i.e. those who play percentage tennis, would be the pushers.

I repeat: Percentage Tennis means choosing the shot at any time within a point that gives you the best possible probability of winning the point later on, given the court position of both you and your opponent and the difficulty of the shot being hit. Implied in this definition is the fact that a large part of percentage tennis is a battle for court positioning. It is easier to create difficulty for an opponent when you are in a relatively better court position. You must learn to be patient in establishing this position. This is so that when you actually decide to finish (hit a winner or create a forced error), the shot is more often a relatively easy one. Here are several examples of good percentage tennis choices:

1) ***A singles player is pushed well behind the baseline on her backhand side. A low flat drive gives her relatively little time to get back into good defensive court position. She needs to play a high crosscourt drive to keep her opponent deep in the court while giving herself time to regain good court positioning.***

2) ***A player is receiving a high defensive lob inside the service box. Depending upon the conditions (wind, sun, etc.) the***

player may elect to let the ball bounce and then go for the put-away overhead. This same high defensive lob, when received near the baseline, should be returned with a ¾ speed placement overhead hit well enough to maintain a small advantage in the point, but not going for a winner. The difference in shot selection in these two cases is all about court geometry and the opponent's reaction times associated with these differing court positions. The different positions suggest different percentage tennis choices.

3) ***A player is facing an opponent with an amazing first serve. Simply getting the ball back in play, even with an underspin lob or bunt, is the "Percentage Tennis" shot in this case. There is at least some probability to win the point later on if the player can get the return back into play. This makes an underspin block the best percentage tennis shot when facing a serve which forces you to lunge for the return.***

The Gear

Knowing which gear to use to play the ball in different situations is crucial for playing good percentage tennis. Gears are typically thought of as in the traditional 5-speed sports-car with 1st gear being the slowest and 5th gear being just below maximum speed (red-lining!). Most tennis matches of high caliber are played with most of the shots in 3rd or 4th gear. Intentionally holding back from 5th gear makes you more consistent, while speeding up from 1st and 2nd gears keeps just enough pressure on your opponent so that he/she cannot control you most of the time and put away easy balls. Against a highly-skilled attacker, however, 1st and 2nd gear shots become an important component of good defense.

As noted above, against a very strong first serve, you may elect simply to block the ball back high and slow in 2nd gear to make the server play the point. However, against his second serve, the election could either be 3rd gear (Steady) or 4th gear (Aggressive) depending upon how you assess your matchup with this particular opponent.

Nick Bollitieri, famous coach of Andre Agassi, Jim Courier and others, has promoted an attack, neutral, and defend system where players are trained to recognize the appropriate level of risk associated with various court positions and difficulty of shot. Training in this way provides players with a solid foundation for understanding the basics of Percentage Tennis.

Court Position and Gear Selection

This diagram illustrates the most simple gear selection system. Any short ball inside the service line should be attacked (green) in 4th gear. Any ball behind the service line and in front of the baseline (yellow) should be played in 3rd gear (neutral). And any ball behind the baseline should be played defensively (red) in 2nd or 3rd gear. The height of the incoming ball is assumed to be anywhere between knee and shoulder height and hit with average pace.

As you improve in level, more of the court becomes green.

The Transition from Defense to Offense

Playing Percentage Tennis often means transitioning gradually, i.e., over the course of two or three shots, from defense to offense. Counter-attacking an opponent's strong shot is usually a recipe for an unforced error. You are far better off playing a defensive shot against a very strong one, following that with a neutral ball or two, and then making the transition to offense if necessary. In this illustration, it's important for Player Blue to get on offense.

Your opponent hits an offensive forehand to pull you off of the court. You should counter with a high looping deep drive which should get you back to neutral. If your 3rd gear shots are solid, you should be able to transition to offense later in the point.

Percentage Tennis: an Illustration

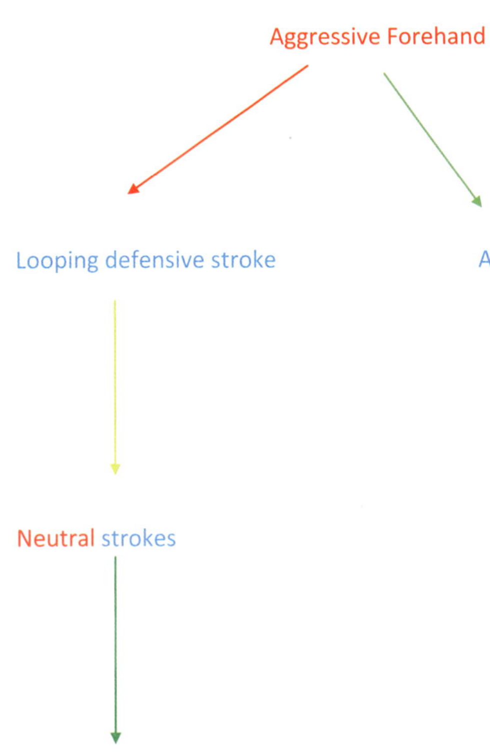

Player Red plays an aggressive forehand to begin the point. Player Blue may respond with either an aggressive forehand or a defensive looping shot. The defensive looping shot transitions him into a neutral rally. Out of this neutral position, Player Blue transitions one more time to offense at the end of the point. Since attacking a short ball is easier than attacking a strong shot, this is the percentage tennis series of shots which should be chosen by Player Blue.

Aggressive stroke

The story behind Percentage Tennis: an Illustration is that there are an indeterminate number of shots exchanged in neutral or 3rd gear until Player Red hits the ball short. It's at this moment that Player Blue transitions to offense.

This diagram speaks to the importance of consistent depth in 3rd gear. If you have this capability, you will force your opponent to attack when it's a lower percentage play. If she cannot match your solid baseline play, then she will not be very successful. As I mentioned in the Introduction, a 2% improvement in the percentage of points won can have an enormous impact on the outcome of a match. Understanding when to go for more or less on your shots is an important component of this 2% improvement.

Tennis Geometry

Percentage Tennis is strongly linked to Court Geometry. This means having a firm grasp of when to hit cross court or down-the-line and when to use angles.

The closer to the net that a player is standing, the easier it is to make virtually every shot – the one exception being a very low ball which is extremely close to the net. This is one of the Immutable Laws of Tennis. If you violate this law too often, you will come in second. Making shots from closer to the net is easier because:

1) The net is less of a factor. Since any opponent must hit the ball up and over the net in order to execute a successful shot, the closer to the net that a player can contact the ball, the better chance that he will get a ball above the level of the net. This means that the net becomes less of a factor when he is executing a shot. For example, visualize an easy overhead with the ball only one foot from the net. This is the proverbial "slam dunk" overhead where execution is easy.

2) It is easier to create angles. Here again visualization will demonstrate the basic principle. The deft touch and short angles of top doubles players when all four players are at the net are marvelous to watch, but these same shots are virtually impossible to make from the baseline position.

3) It is easier to hit any target when a player is closer to the target. Just as in darts or basketball, it is easier to hit targets when a player is closer. As a basketball player would you rather be attempting to make a layup or a 3-point shot if $1 million were on the line? This also means, all other things being equal, that a ball struck from closer to the net will give an opponent less time to react. Getting "close enough" is what gives a player the opportunity to attack and create forced errors and winners. So, any game plan should look to exploit these basic

advantages of moving forward into the court: easier to hit targets, easier to create angles, and easier to create reaction time problems for an opponent.

Look at the following statistics from the Djokovic-Nadal Australian Open final of 2012, one of the greatest matches of all time. These statistics all speak to the importance of superior court position.

> ***Djokovic, who had superior court position because he took the return of serve sooner, hit 36 groundstroke winners (28 forehand/8 backhand) while Nadal hit 25 groundstroke winners (20 forehand/5 backhand). It was easier for Djokovic to hit winners because he was closer to the baseline. In the third set, which Djokovic won 6-2, he made contact with the ball 64 percent of the time behind the baseline and 34 percent inside. This is truly remarkable court position. Conversely, Nadal made contact 96 percent of the time behind the baseline and only 4 percent of the time from inside the baseline. Because of this, Nadal won only two points returning serve and only hit two winners for the set.***

As a consequence of Tennis Geometry, you should devote more time in training to developing competence in the forecourt. Most players prefer the backcourt and there is no doubt that they can achieve a solid level of competence playing this type of game. One need only look to Harold Solomon, a top-level baseliner from the late 1970's who was ranked in the Top 5 in the world. However, it is Bjorn Borg, also a top-level baseliner from that era whom we remember. This is because he developed the ability to attack the net at opportune moments. (Well, of course, he also won a few Grand Slams!). Borg was a master at exploiting the basics of Court Geometry.

Drills involving half-volleys, taking the ball on the rise, returning serve from inside the baseline (like Serena Williams!), and picking off high looping balls with swing volleys are all important components of the Tennis Geometry piece of the puzzle.

For example, if you routinely stand a foot behind the baseline to return serve against a certain player, you should return at or slightly inside the baseline in practice in order to improve your reaction time and preparation. A similar theme is emphasized when players drill with additional rules such as "you cannot back up behind the baseline." These drills improve half-volley and playing-the-ball-on the-rise skills.

Tennis Geometry

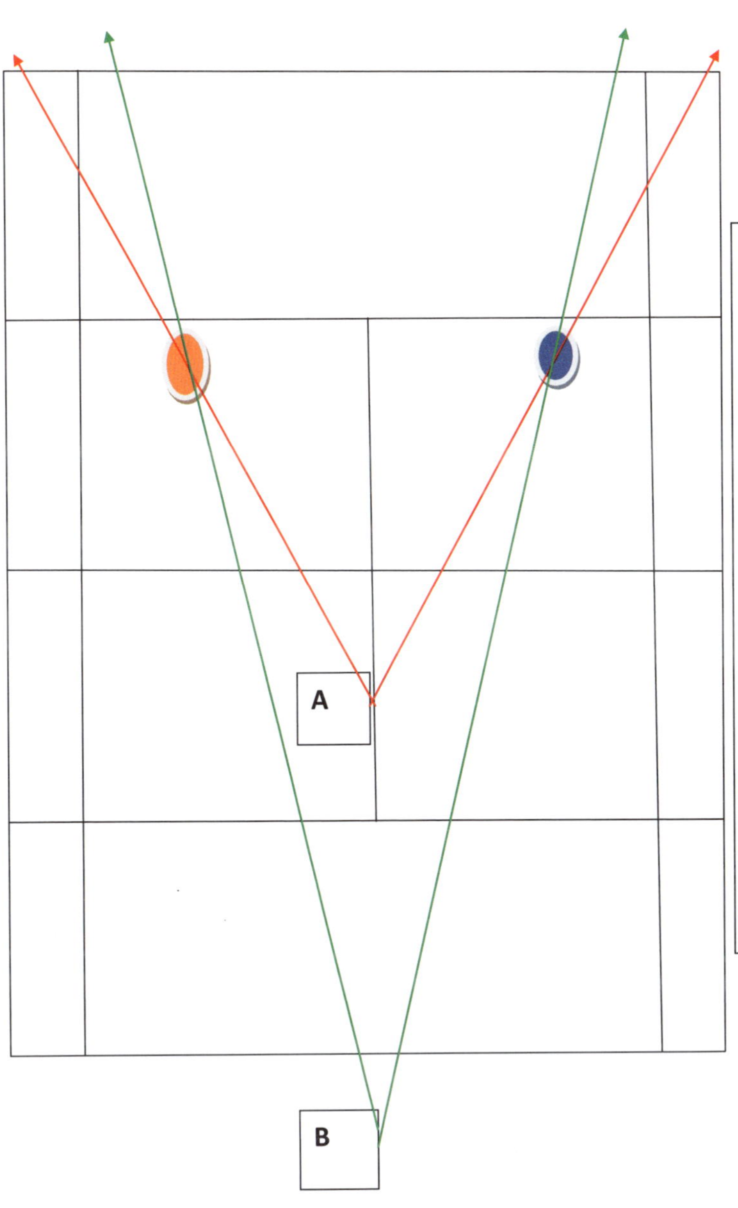

Player A is closer to the blue oval making it easier to hit this target. Because he is closer, there is also less reaction time for his opponent and his shot has a sharper angle. Compare the path of A's shot (the red lines) with B's shot (the green lines). This sharper angle may also be hit to the opposite side of the court through the orange oval. If the distance between the red and green arrows is measured at the opponent's baseline, it's clear that Player A has the potential to make his opponent do much more running AND give him less time to get into position.

Court Positioning

Good court position enables you to make it as difficult as possible for your opponent to hit winners or get you off balance. You must learn to recover to the place in the court which will bisect (cut in half) the possible returns of the opponent. This minimizes the distance that you have to move in order to get to an opponent's best shot, a shot near either of the sidelines. See Diagram: Court Positioning.

This is also the reason that most groundstrokes in tennis are played either cross court or down the middle. Playing groundstrokes with this pattern makes it easier to get to an excellent recovery position without having to move very far. See Diagram: Baseline Positioning – Shot Selection.

The opposite is true when a player is volleying in singles. Now the put-away volley is cross court and the consistency volley is down the line. The down the line volley minimizes the recovery distance and should be used when there is no opening to hit the cross court winner. See Diagram: Forecourt Positioning – Shot Selection.

A 4.0 female singles player was practicing with me and she played many down the line backhand groundstrokes. My response was to hit cross court forehands, the easiest shot in tennis. I saw her a few days later and she said: "I couldn't walk for two days," i.e., she did all of the running. This is what I mean about violating an Immutable Law of Tennis. It will not work!

Court Positioning

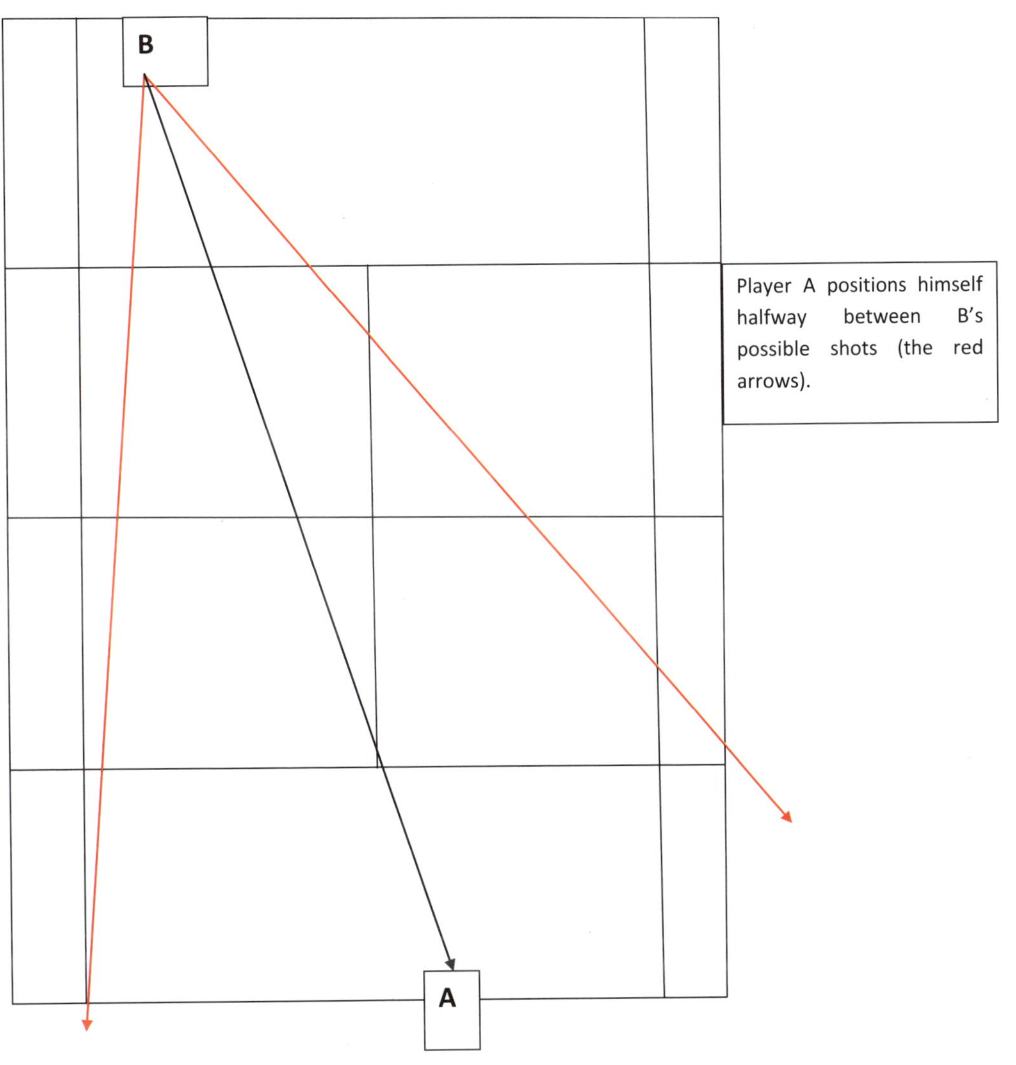

Baseline Positioning – Shot Selection

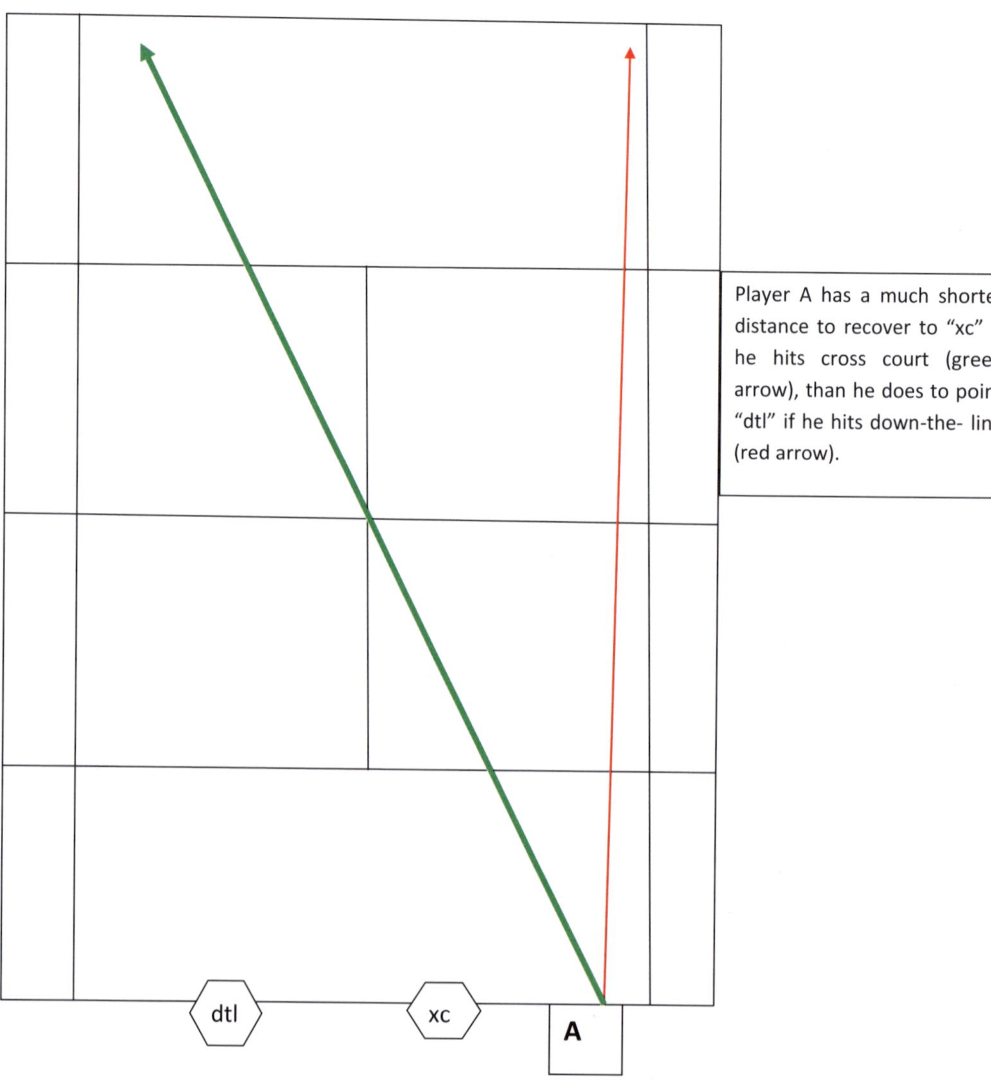

Forecourt positioning – Shot Selection

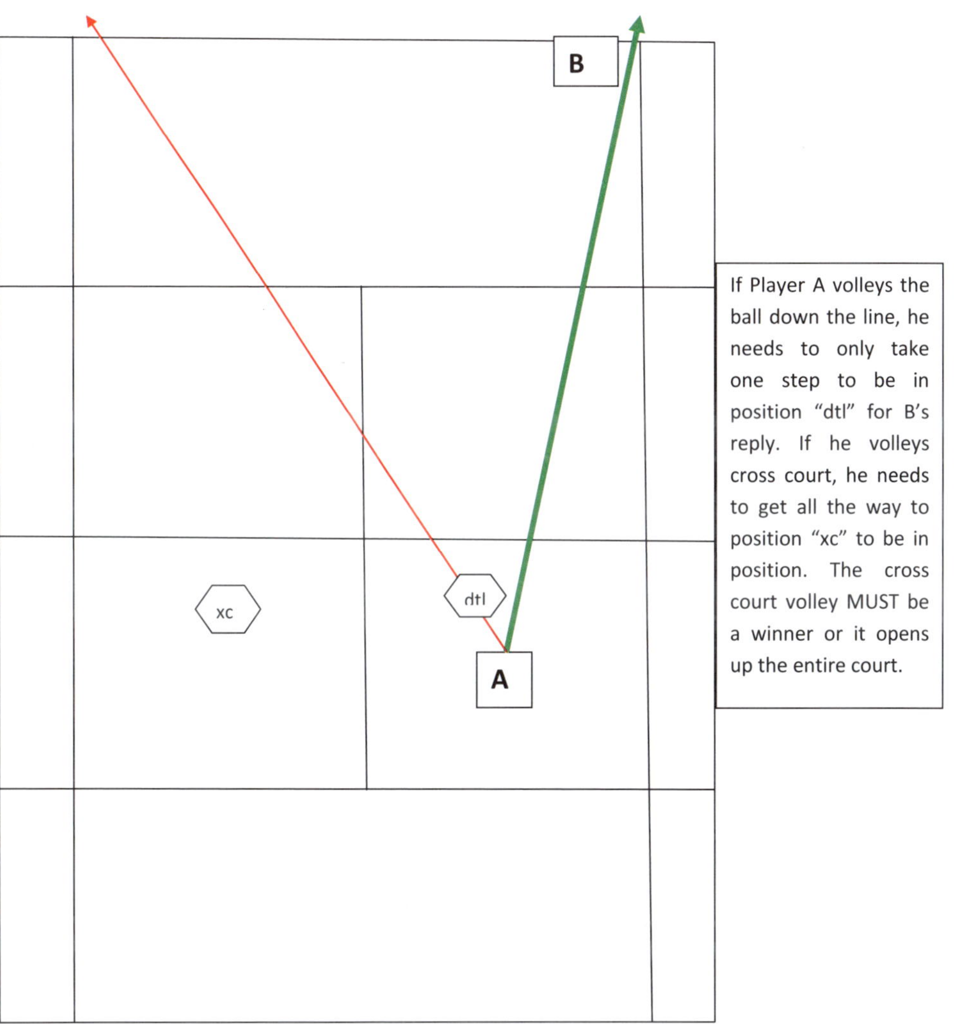

If Player A volleys the ball down the line, he needs to only take one step to be in position "dtl" for B's reply. If he volleys cross court, he needs to get all the way to position "xc" to be in position. The cross court volley MUST be a winner or it opens up the entire court.

Building Your Game

Because of the Immutable Laws of Tennis, there is a necessary foundation upon which you MUST build your own game in order to become an effective all-court player. The Tactical Pyramid below shows the hierarchy of attributes which your game must possess in order to become a strong player.

The Tactical Pyramid

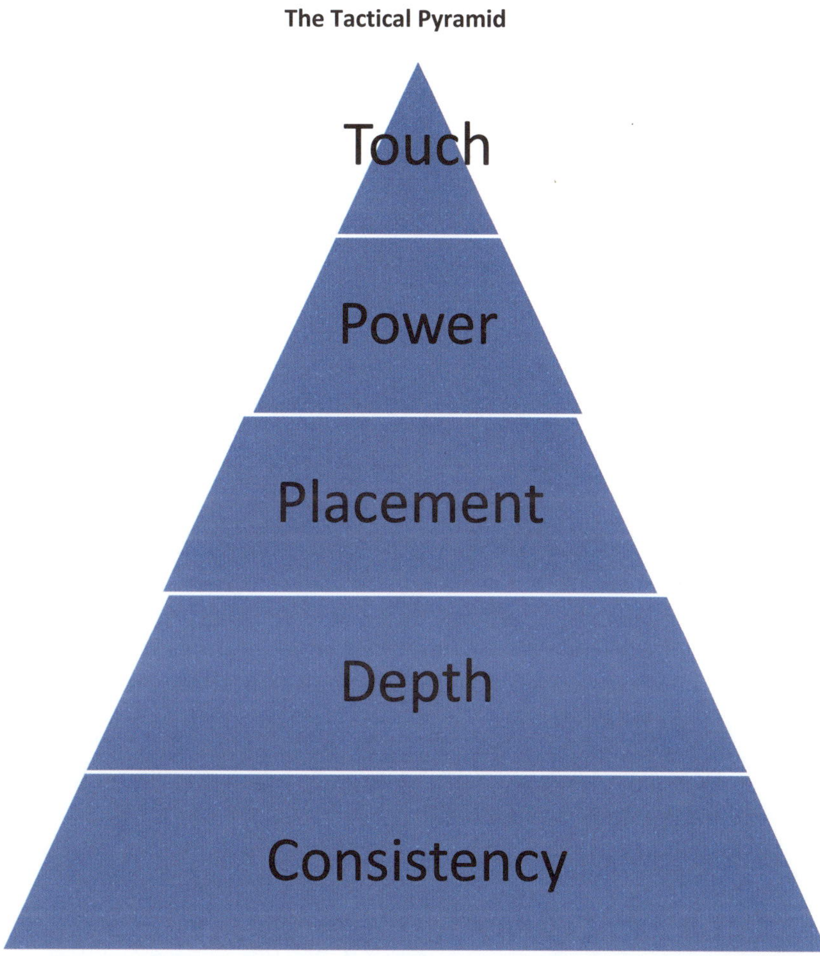

As I noted in the Introduction, unforced errors are the bane of a tennis player's existence. Too many unforced errors make it nearly impossible to win a match. This is true even at the top levels of tennis. At the 2014 French Open, six of the eight quarterfinal matches in the men's singles were won by the player who committed fewer unforced errors. Hence, Consistency is at the base of the Tactical Pyramid.

Because reaction time and court coverage are integral to defending your own court, the next step in the Pyramid is Depth. As you just saw in the section on Tennis Geometry, you will also cut down on your opponent's ability to make angles, i.e. run you into submission, if you can maintain depth on your strokes. Ideally, you would want the first two steps to work together – you are able consistently to keep the ball deep.

Next, your ability to place the ball to all parts of the court should be added to your game. From midcourt, you should be able to attack anywhere at all and from the baseline you need to be able to dip the ball low if your opponent is attacking the net. This is important on the serve as well, where a ¾- speed serve to the weaker side of an opponent is usually superior to a more powerful shot hit into his strength.

After Placement has been developed, adding Power to your targets will be a plus since this reduces the reaction time of your opponent. This means gradually adding more pace to all of your shots, whether it is your first serve or your 3rd gear rally ball from the baseline. Just a small improvement in your power can have a meaningful effect on your ability to penetrate your opponent's defenses. As we saw above, playing in the correct "gear" is an important component of playing good tennis.

Finally, a complete "touch" game which includes the ability to hit drop shots and drop volleys to expose the short part of the court should be developed. This is the finishing step and with it, you have become the complete all-court player.

Inverting the Pyramid

If your Tactical Pyramid is out of whack, it means that it will have corrosive effects on the rest of your game. In the Pyramid pictured below, a player has developed her game around her touch, i.e. she plays drop shots frequently and well, but does not have the ability to play the ball deep in a consistent manner. Her ability to use Power is not supported by a solid foundation. This has an immediate effect on her ability to play against a balanced opponent.

An Inverted Pyramid

Her game crumbles without a solid foundation.

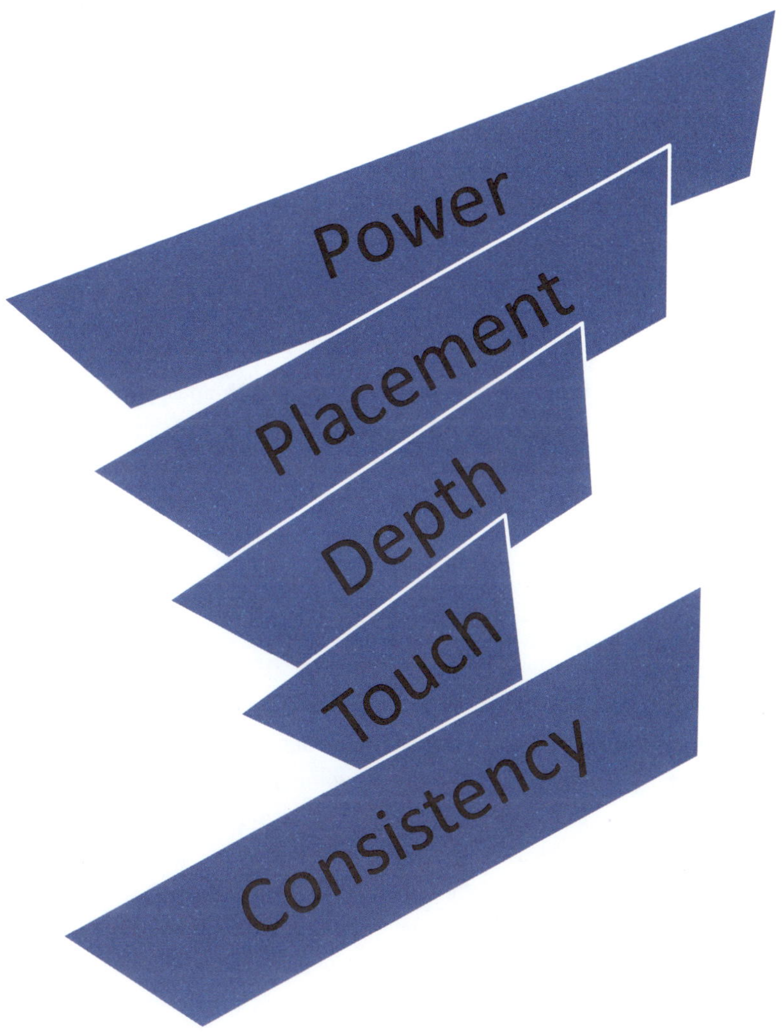

Benoit Paire, a talented Frenchman, who currently (end of 2015) ranks #19 in the world, has a game built upon just such an Inverted Pyramid. He can drop shot beautifully from almost anywhere at any time, but his forehand depth and consistency are not up to the standards of the top players.

Playing in the correct gear may also be viewed through the Steady/Aggressive lens. Depending upon the score and your opponent, you should decide if your best chance to win the match comes from playing a Steady game or taking more risk, i.e. playing an Aggressive game. The gear associated with this decision will most likely vary.

The Steady/Aggressive Lens

The dominant question of any strategic matchup with an opponent should be framed by this simple question: If I play Steady, i.e. solid 3rd gear shots, is this good enough to defeat my opponent? If the answer is yes, then playing your shots consistently deep (the bottom two steps on the foundation of the Pyramid!) will be your best strategy. There is no need for you to take unnecessary risk. This explains why some matches at the professional level may seem boring. Pros understand this and sometimes winning a match is no more than just "another routine day at the office."

For simplicity, let's say that both you and your opponent may choose to play a given point either in Steady or Aggressive mode. By definition, Aggressive mode means that each of you is hitting more winners, but also making more unforced errors than you are in Steady mode. Let us also define your "underlying abilities" as the percentage of point-ending shots being either winners or errors for each of you in both modes. It is then possible to choose the mode (Steady or Aggressive) which gives you the best chance at victory. This is not a calculation which top players actually make. However, just like the Win-Skill grid, they do make decisions regarding their risk-taking *as if* these calculations were being made. The point here is that making the actual calculations proves that the intuition is correct.

The payoffs or rewards, depending upon the choices which you and your opponent make, result in four different payoffs -- each of you can play in either Steady or Aggressive mode. In our example, Players #1 and #2 have the following "underlying abilities", i.e. the percentage of total shots which result in point-ending shots hit in either their Steady or Aggressive modes. Remember, players always make more winners and more unforced errors in their Aggressive mode.

	Steady 1	Agg 1	Steady 2	Agg 2
Winners	0.05	0.10	0.04	0.10
Errors	0.02	0.08	0.02	0.06

This is a fairly high-level match as only 4% of total shots are unforced errors in Steady mode –i.e., each makes point-ending unforced errors on 2% of his shots). Player #1 is a bit better at hitting winners in this mode (5% > 4%). In Aggressive mode, they both make more errors, but also more winners. While their ability to hit winners in this mode is equal (10% = 10%), Player #1 does make more unforced errors (8% > 6%) in Aggressive mode.

I think we should expect that the best choices would be for Player #1 to choose Steady and Player #2 to choose Aggressive because Player #2 intuits that, while he is consistent, Player #1 is even better in this mode. In the payoff matrix below, the payoffs are the probabilities that each player will win a point in a given mode. Each player is naturally trying to maximize these probabilities for himself.

Here are the actual payoffs[5]:

	Player 2	Steady	Aggressive
Player 1	Steady	.545, .455	.484, .516
	Aggressive	.508, .492	.479, .521

[5] M. Daniele Paserman, *Gender Differences in Performance in Competitive Environments? Evidence from Professional Tennis Players,* Boston University, January 2010, unpublished paper. Prof. Paserman develops a strategic model of tennis using a Soft/Aggressive framework. The formulas for the payoff probabilities, number of unforced errors, and rally length all follow from his strategic model.

Player #1's payoffs are listed first in each entry. For example, his payoff from being Steady, if Player #2 is also Steady, is .545. This means that, given their underlying abilities, Player #1 has a 54.5% probability of winning the point if they both play Steady. Player #2's payoffs are listed second. If he also plays Steady, his payoff is .455. However, Player #2 only has a chance to win the match if he plays Aggressive (both .516 and .521 are greater than .5). Therefore, we know that Player #2 should choose to be Aggressive. Our intuition was correct! The best strategic option for both players is highlighted in red. This match will (or should, if #2 plays with courage!) see many points of the Steady (Player #1)/Aggressive (Player #2) type.

Notice that Player #1's better option is to be Steady, but this will still lose him the match! Here is a clear example of how Player #2's courage to be Aggressive can win him a match which he would lose for sure if he were content to lay back and play Steady.

And here are two other interesting facts! Given the "underlying abilities" of the players and their simple choice of being Steady or Aggressive, it is possible also to calculate the percentage of points which end in unforced errors and the average rally length. If both players were to play Steady, the percentage of points ending in an unforced error would be about 31% as compared with 42% when Player #2 correctly plays in Aggressive mode. Player #2 must be willing to miss a few in order to win! In addition the average rally length decreases from over 15 shots per point to just fewer than 8.

> ***Players who come out of a match and say: "It was an amazing match! It lasted over 3 hours and every point was a battle but I came up just short. Next time, I'll win it!" are not going to make any progress. These players need to develop their offensive weapons.***

It's also important that you grasp exactly what I mean by being Steady. It is more than simply getting the ball back. If you slow down your rally ball to 2nd gear, your opponent will have the time to set up and play her best offense. The

3rd gear shot which you should attempt to develop should be deep and heavy enough to send the following message: IF YOU ATTACK ME WHEN I'VE HIT THIS SHOT, YOU WILL BE OUTSIDE OF YOUR COMFORT ZONE. IF YOU ARE OUTSIDE OF YOUR COMFORT ZONE TOO OFTEN, YOU WILL MISS TOO MUCH AND I WILL WIN THE MATCH.

Your ability to access your correct gear will be a big factor in your tennis success. As you approach the close of a match, match pressure increases. Frequently, this increased match pressure takes players out of their correct gears, i.e., players of all levels either begin to over hit or push the ball. Clemson coach Chuck Kriese calls the former going for a "Chainsaw Killing." And I will name the latter "Holding on for Dear Life."

As mentioned above, the gear of any given stroke may be thought of as ranging from 1-5 as in a standard stick shift car. Most groundstrokes should be struck in 3rd or 4th gear depending upon the situation. Here are a few examples.

A forehand approach shot should typically be hit in 4th gear – the player is in good control of his balance and inside the baseline. It is necessary to maintain reaction time pressure on the opponent.

A more subtle example would be on the return of serve. Recently, I was playing a doubles match where I was the weakest player on the court. My job on the return was to keep the ball in play, away from any poacher, and hopefully get my partner involved in the point. I was very successful, but my team was getting beaten because all of my returns, while low, were hit in 2nd gear. This allowed the serve-and-volleyer time to stop in midcourt and lineup an aggressive groundstroke with which he pinned me to the baseline. I was not able to get my (very strong) partner into the point. While I was doing my job (getting the ball in play), things were not working. I resolved, for the next day's rematch, to hit all of my returns with a minimum of

3rd gear with some forehands in 4th. Now the serve-and-volleyer was forced to play a half-volley, my partner was able to get in the game, and I got much better looks at my next shot. We did exceedingly well with this despite the fact that I now missed some returns because I was raising the gear.

This is a concrete example of the Steady/Aggressive payoffs which you just read about and it highlights the key idea behind playing Percentage Tennis. Percentage Tennis means choosing the appropriate target/gear such that your chances of winning the point are maximized. It does NOT mean making every shot. From the example above, you can clearly see how making every shot was NOT my best Percentage Tennis choice. In this example, I did not change my plan, but I did adjust my gear. The big picture did not change – I needed a way to get my partner into the match – and I needed to be more Aggressive in order to do so.

At crucial times in a match, players often slow down their attacking gear and then wonder what happened – Holding on for Dear Life. You must know your proper gear and stick to it! Looking at a 60/40 split (a very one-sided match) is extremely informative when it comes to choosing the correct gear.

Let's say that a returner in doubles gets 10 attackable 2nd serves in a set. If she returns in 4th gear, she will miss 3/10 approaches, but of the remaining 7, she will win 6 either by directly forcing errors from her opponent or setting up either herself or her partner for relatively easy finishes from the net. Alternatively, let's say that the same returner bunts all 10 approaches in and runs to the net, only now the server has adequate time to prepare her response. The server hits 6/10 well placed shots, either lobs or passing shots, which lead to winning the point. The better team has now lost the match by playing in the wrong gear (typically a slower or scared gear).

Making the correct Steady/Aggressive choice lies at the foundation of making an effective game plan. Here are the choices which you should make depending upon how you match up with your opponent. Each of these imagined matchups is against the same player.

1) You are Steadier when you both play in Steady mode. You should choose Steady. As mentioned above, this is the simplest and easiest way to win a match. A possible switch to Aggressive might be in order if endurance is a factor, however.
2) You play Steady and your opponent plays Aggressive. Many times, remaining Steady will still win you the match as his flashy winners are more than compensated for by more unforced errors. However, sometimes you may need to switch to Aggressive if his attacking game is effective.
3) You play Aggressive either because your opponent is better in Steady mode than you are or because his Aggressive mode is exceptional and you need to get him on the defensive at least some of the time.

Here's how I work this paradigm. I begin the match Steady (3rd gear) knowing that unforced errors by my opponent will lead to him handing me the lead (he's playing in 4th gear). However, no top player will tolerate beating himself, so at some point he will revert to Steady mode. As soon as he does, I change to 4th gear and overwhelm his Steady game. He senses this and switches back to 4th gear. But I feel this, revert to Steady mode and once again, his errors start piling up …

Or, imagine that the better doubles team has gotten the lead by playing in the correct gear, but as the match remains close, i.e., the points become more important, they begin to take pace off of their approaches. They have given the opposition a chance at victory without the other team having to do anything differently! If you are winning with Aggressive, then stay Aggressive!

From the point of view of Court Geometry, here is another way of looking at any matchup ...

The Most Basic Geometric Matchup

Recall from our discussion of Court Geometry that playing cross court groundstrokes forms the foundation of defending your own side of the net. Very simply (when either two righties or two lefties meet), there are only two such patterns of play: 1) backhand to backhand cross court; or 2) forehand to forehand cross court. Your most basic tactical decision is to assess which of these diagonals is the better matchup for you against any given opponent. Let's look at this in more detail:

Backhand-to-backhand matchup: If your backhand is Steadier than your opponent's, then you should play this pattern all day long. This will force your opponent to become more Aggressive with her backhand by either hitting harder or changing the direction to down the line. Hitting harder could lead to more errors from her, while hitting down the line could open up her court if she fails to play it Aggressively enough. This is the simplest way to win a match if your backhand is more Steady than your opponent's.

Kei Nishikori employs this tactic again and again. It was good enough to beat Novak Djokovic in the 2014 US Open semis.

Backhand- to- backhand matchup (part 2): If your opponent plays her backhand down the line in response to being less Steady than you are, then you need to play a solid cross court forehand into the middle of the open court. This will keep her on the run and not allow her to set up for her forehand stroke. Occasionally you should return her down the line backhand with a down the line forehand. This will keep her from recovering too quickly to cover the open court. As you will see below, this is simply another application of the idea that the optimal strategy is a mixed strategy. To be clear: the mix in this case is something like 80/20 in favor of hitting the open court.

Forehand- to- Forehand matchup: All of the Steady backhand-to- backhand principles apply with the proviso that most players can be more naturally Aggressive with their forehands and are also capable of changing direction and hitting well down the line somewhat better from this wing. This can still be an effective way to use Court Geometry to win; it is, however, a bit more unpredictable than the backhand- to-backhand matchup.

Forehand-to-Forehand matchup (part 2): Similarly, if your opponent plays her forehand down the line in response to being less consistent than you are along the forehand diagonal, then you need to play a solid cross court backhand into the middle of the open court. Your opponent is now in a pickle. Either she plays a cross court backhand (not good for her because you are more Steady along the backhand diagonal) or she plays down the line and you keep her on the run by playing into the open court.

> ***This tactic has been employed to beat Stan Wawrinka, the 2015 French Open champion, earlier in his career. However, as his forehand has improved, it's become more and more difficult to use this tactic against him.***

Now that we have established the Steady/Aggressive foundation of a good game plan and seen how Court Geometry can be used to refine that plan, let's look at the tactics used to implement the plan of your choice.

Tactics

The tactics used in any particular match are the specific tools which you use to dismantle your opponent. If you have assessed that your opponent is better at Steady than you are, then a list of possible tactics would look like this:

Attack any reasonable mid-court ball

Take any floating balls out of the air

Use drop shots to disrupt your opponent's comfort at the baseline

Chip and charge or return with pace against his second serve

Serve and volley occasionally

The choices and frequency of tactics you would choose would depend upon how your strengths match up against your opponent's weaknesses. This involves an assessment of your opponent and I will discuss this next.

Sizing Up An Opponent

Now that you have a firmer grasp of the Immutable Laws of Tennis and the tactics which could be employed to implement your plan, it is important to add another ingredient to making a game plan: assessing your opponent's strengths and weaknesses. This consists of three parts:

1) Physical assessment of one's opponent

2) Technical assessment of one's opponent

3) Court surface and playing conditions

These assessments also require practice and experience. Ultimately they must be internalized so that they are readily accessible when making a game plan and assessing how well that plan is being carried out. Numbers 1 and 2 are assessed in the warm-up or by scouting; i.e. there are tactics which are high percentage against Opponent A that simply don't work against Opponent B.

I recently began a singles program for 4.0/4.5 women at my club. I play each week to help them to develop their games. One of the players has a particularly good forehand drop shot which she disguises very well by taking a full swing at the ball. My initial physical assessment was that she was not a great mover, so when she hit a drop, I played a re-drop. Weakness exposed!

Physical Assessment

Immediately upon meeting your opponent, you should do a preliminary assessment of his physical assets and liabilities. Age, height, and weight are three of the basic things which should be assessed. For example, younger, stronger players will most likely want to hit harder and eschew the lob. They will also be prone to more unforced errors. Within the gear management paradigm discussed above, I would be choosing to play more Steady points as opposed to Aggressive points against this younger stronger opponent. I would still want to be aggressive but would need to choose my moments carefully. Similarly, a shorter opponent would be more vulnerable to a lob and a taller opponent more vulnerable to balls at their feet. And finally, a heavier opponent should be treated in the same manner as a player with limited mobility.

Often physical liabilities are easily recognized because one's opponent is wearing some kind of brace, bandage, or other assorted injury paraphernalia on his body. The most obvious example of this is a player with a large cumbersome knee brace. A well-designed game plan should immediately attempt to put the court coverage abilities of this type of opponent under stress -- particularly up and back movement and quick changes of direction.

Your physical assessment should happen not only with respect to quickness and court coverage but also with respect to endurance. If you are fast AND you have excellent endurance, you can send a strong message back to your opponent that he will need to thread the needle repeatedly in order to beat you. In this case, you would choose to play Steady in the framework which we developed above.

> ***A former Division I college volleyball player took up tennis three years ago at my club. She has made outstanding progress because she is an excellent athlete. Although I continue to want her to do it more efficiently, she sends a clear message in her singles matches: "I will get every ball and I will get it for 3 hours. Come and beat me if you can!"***

As the level of play rises, the physical weaknesses become more difficult to spot. It is no longer a question of your opponent being slow, but slow *relative* to your speed. Even at the top levels of tennis, where all players move well and hit hard, there are still differences in quickness and power between players. The Top 4 men in the world (Federer, Nadal, Djokovic, and Murray) all distinguish themselves from the field with their movement, court coverage, and endurance.

Technical Assessment

During the warm-up, you should look for any anomaly in your opponent's technique. This begins with checking out his grips on the various strokes. Any extreme grip suggests a potential specific weakness. Extreme grips are those which exist at or over the margin of what is generally thought to be acceptable. The following chart should help you to understand which grips are associated with certain weaknesses on all of the strokes.

The first column lists the stroke; the second lists the type of extreme grip; the third lists a (simple!) description of the weakness.

Stroke:	**Grip:**	**Weakness:**
Forehand	Western Continental	Low balls High balls
Backhand 1-handed	Continental	high balls
Backhand 2-handed	Full Eastern with dominant hand	low balls
Fh volley:	Eastern fh or Western grip Eastern bh	low balls high balls - inability to generate pace
Bh volley:	2-handed volley Continental	Insufficient reach Lacks power
Serve:	Fh groundstroke grip Extreme bh grip	Cannot create enough spin Too much spin - not enough pace

For example, a Continental grip on the forehand drive would suggest a weakness with high balls and might even force this player to slice a high forehand. Similarly, a Western style grip on the forehand volley would suggest a weakness with balls having to be played from below a player's knees.

Having this skill can save you a significant amount of time when it comes to designing a game plan. Rather than waiting five or six games to discover how to play against a particular opponent, the match can begin with a strong suspicion of where a potential weakness lies.

There are innumerable tennis books which provide clear pictures of the various grips. I am not going to repeat these pictures here. Suffice it to say that being able to identify an opponent's grips can be of enormous value when developing a game plan. Learning to spot these grips is well worth your time and effort.

The spin created on each of the shots should also be noted. While topspin is virtually universal at the top levels of tennis, many accomplished club-level players do not create topspin. Generally, this type of player should be attacked by rushing the net as he will be unable to consistently "dip" the ball at your feet.

Years ago, I played against an opponent who played for one of the Big Ten universities. He was a big-time aggressor, but he had a side-spin forehand. I was convinced in the warm-up that this would prove to be a liability because its trajectory would take it too close to the top of the net. I was down a set and 5-4 with him serving for the match before the weakness showed itself with a few unforced errors into the net. Game, set, match, Schewior!

And finally, the gear with which an opponent warms up is also a part of the assessment process. Players who consistently either under-hit or over-power the ball are sending you a strong message that they will not be able to play the pressure moments with the correct level of pace and /or consistency.

The toughest opponents to play are those who present no apparent weaknesses, either physical or technical. In this case, there are no shortcuts and your understanding of Tennis Geometry, Court Positioning, and Percentage Tennis will all come into play.

Playing Conditions

Alterations to your basic game plan should be made based upon the playing conditions. These include court surface, indoor vs. outdoor, the sun and wind, and the crowd. As a general rule, more difficult conditions suggest playing with a greater margin of error – hitting higher over the net and not hitting near the sidelines. Avoiding unforced errors becomes even more crucial in these situations.

Conversely, indoor and/or faster courts and a home crowd suggest going for somewhat more, i.e. tilting the Steady/Aggressive Lens in the Aggressive direction. At the professional level, where the margins are so slim, a slight change in court speed can have a large effect on the success of certain tactics.

Early in 2015, Roger Federer was able successfully to attack Novak Djokovic at both Dubai and Cincinnati, relatively fast hard courts. At the year-end championships in London, the slightly slower court speed dulled his attack and Djokovic went on to victory.

Three Simple Rules

These simple rules will also be of some help when making game plans and adjustments to game plans. Keep them in mind.

Rule #1: BARELY WINNING IS OFTEN GOOD ENOUGH TO WIN. You should try to match up the patterns that get you over 50% of the points won. Even a 52-48 advantage translates into a 20% greater probability of winning a match when compared to a 50/50 split in points won or lost. Many times finding this 52%

pattern means that you must be willing to accept some errors along with your good shots. Failure to do so will mean that you end up playing too safely.

Rule #2: NEVER CHANGE A WINNING GAME. This adage has been around in tennis for a long time and remains true.

> ***Here's an example from the 2012 Sony Ericsson Open played in Miami. In the 4th round, Victoria Azarenka (on a 22-match winning streak) played the #16 seed Dominica Cibulkova. Cibulkova led 6-1, 5-1 when she changed her game. She had built her lead by taking a very high level of risk, particularly when returning the 2nd serve. These returns were placed right in the corners at extremely high pace. However, at closing time, she became more conservative on her returns. The points on her service games also became longer. Cibulkova changed her game and Azarenka came back to win 1-6, 7-6, 7-5.***

Rule #3: USE A WINNING PLAY UNTIL AN OPPONENT ADOPTS A SUCCESSFUL COUNTER-MEASURE. If he doesn't – just keep using it. This principle is really just a sub-rule of Principle #2. Here's an example of failing to use this rule.

> ***An example from my good friend, the highly-talented, Peter Bromley: Peter, an excellent serve- and- volley player, was matched up against a French Open doubles winner (Eric Fromm) in singles. Eric had a big-time forehand. Peter built up a 4-1 lead by attacking his backhand relentlessly. At this point, I had to leave the site to play a match elsewhere. I returned a couple of hours later only to find out that Peter had lost the match. I asked him what happened and he said: "I mixed in some serves to his forehand and he hit some spectacular returns." My question was a simple WHY? A football team who can't stop the opposition from running the ball time after time for a first down is doomed to lose. Similarly, a tennis player who can't defend with his backhand should never be let off the hook by mixing***

things up. This is a flawed game plan and does not force the opponent to make any adjustments whatsoever.

Implementing a successful game plan means knowing how to match up your strengths with your opponent's weaknesses while at the same time adhering to solid court positioning and committing to playing percentage tennis.

Violating any of The Immutable Laws of Tennis will get you into trouble!

Here is an example from shot selection, in this case poor shot selection resulting from not understanding basic court position: A doubles player just loves to attack the opposing net player with down the line drives from the baseline. She attempts this shot about seven times per set and hits two outstanding winners while losing the other five points either to her errors or the volleyer's placements down the middle. If her coach could convince her to go down the line only twice per set, and she splits the other five points 50/50, this would yield the 2% improvement needed to change the match outcome.

As underscored in the quotation from *The Art of War* which began this chapter, the stubbornness of this player who is sticking with a bad idea has doomed her to coming in second in most of her matches. A process-based approach would allow her to make the adjustments necessary for victory. Don't let yourself be this player!

Starting the Point

Before the start of each point, you should choose BOTH a target and a gear. The shot selection at the start of a point is intricately connected to the way in which you visualize yourself winning the point.

What I mean by the target is obvious – both the server and receiver should be choosing their targets before the start of the point. Since the returner is uncertain if she will have a forehand or a backhand, she should choose a target for either possibility. In doubles, both the server's and receiver's partners should also be reminding themselves of their basic responsibilities before the start of each point.

Thinking Backwards or Backwards Induction

Let me repeat what I just said above: THE SHOT SELECTION AT THE START OF A POINT IS INTRICATELY CONNECTED TO THE WAY IN WHICH YOU VISUALIZE YOURSELF WINNING THE POINT. Lewis Carroll once said: "If you don't know where you're going, any road will get you there." Similarly, in tennis, if you don't have a clear vision of both the type of point you'd like to play (Steady or Aggressive) and/or how you'd like the point to end, each of the shots chosen along the way will lack a clear purpose.

Playing to an opponent's weakness is a key element in devising a successful game plan. At the lower levels of competitive tennis, this can be fairly simple. As I mentioned above, a default game plan such as "attack his backhand relentlessly" will often succeed. Even at the top levels of tennis, this can work against certain players.

> ***Here's a repeat of a previously mentioned example: Marc Lopez, who is the occasional doubles partner of Rafael Nadal, has a potent forehand and an average backhand. The top pros control him by serving 90% ¾-speed first serves to his backhand. He knows that it's coming, but he can't do much to stop it.***

Sometimes it is not this simple however. Your opponent also has the ability to adjust and prepare for any pattern which is constantly repeated. It is not unreasonable to assume that, if he knows that you are serving to his backhand, he will begin to return serve better off of that side because he is ready for that shot alone. This means that, as a server, it is important to create some doubt as to where you are going to serve the ball. Research has shown that returners get better when the previous serve was placed to the same spot. This provides support for the idea that the optimal strategy is to mix your serves "just enough" against players who are capable of adjusting[6].

Thinking Backwards – Some Examples

Here are some examples of how to use Backwards Induction to fine tune your game plan and shot selection.

> ***A clear example of using "Backwards Induction" comes from comparing my playing style when I was in my late 20s with my playing style now. My goal in my 20s was to be very patient and solid from the backcourt while at the same time looking to get to the net at every opportunity. Because my goal was to finish at the net, my percentage tennis groundstrokes were deep, but rarely threatening. My court speed and endurance were excellent. Now, that I don't move forward and back nearly as well, I need to create more offense from the backcourt. So, when I get a forehand "look", I nearly always take more risk than I used to. I choose to cover up my lack of speed and endurance with shorter points.***

You may also use Backwards Induction to determine your shot selection. The following example is from mixed doubles, which I consider a truly great game for learning tactics. Because the relative strengths/weaknesses are magnified in mixed doubles, shot selection becomes all the more important in determining the outcome.

> ***My partner and I won a close first set in a tiebreak and led 4-2 with the opposing woman to serve. This is a difficult game to win for our opponents and, at the same time, it was also a MUST win game for them. The opposing man was an aggressive poacher. By backwards induction, I reasoned that he had to***

[6] Joel Wiles, Mixed Strategy Equilibrium in Tennis Serves, Honors Thesis, Duke University, April 2006.

poach on the first point – if he didn't, I would be poaching the next ball from the server. I instructed my partner to return down the line. He moved. We had an easy point. I won my receiving point so it is now 0-30. The score is now all the more desperate for them, so I reasoned that he would be poaching again. Again, he moved and my partner, on instructions, hit a down the line winner. Game, set, match, Schewior. ☺

One final example of using Backwards Induction – this time to make a small adjustment in court positioning:

A strong 4.0 women's doubles pair is fighting gamely, but they are slightly overmatched against a pair of 4.5s. In particular, one of the 4.5s has a strong forehand and has been doing an excellent job of returning serve. However, just as closing time approaches, she misses a few and suddenly slows down her gear. The 4.0s can now make first volleys which were too difficult to make earlier in the match. The 4.0s reach set point at 6-5 on their serve in the tiebreak. Backwards induction led me to reason as follows: 1) the returner will not risk going back to her more aggressive gear as this is an important point and she has recently missed a few; 2) her slower cross- court return was sitting up and making for easy volleys for the server; 3) therefore, she MUST lob the ball. With my best ESP, I sent a telepathic message (haha!) to the net player: you need to play one step further back. She failed to receive the message in time. The lob was slightly behind her as she smashed the ball 2 inches long. Backwards Induction would have had her in perfect position to win the set.

A Mixed Strategy is Optimal

Serving placement in professional tennis has been analyzed to see if the serving choices are rational. [7] In this case "rational" means winning an equal percentage of points whether serving to the forehand or the backhand and randomizing the target choice. Professional tennis is a perfect medium for this analysis because of the high stakes (players will not fool around when playing for large amounts of money). In addition, the years of learning/training which stand behind any professional tennis players make them perfect subjects of investigation. The analysis accounts for the fact that even though a returner's backhand may be weaker than his forehand, his backhand return will improve if he knows to expect a backhand with certainty. Hence, a server will optimally pick on the backhand while mixing in just enough serves to the forehand to keep the returner honest. The mix which provides the greatest success occurs when there are equal percentages of points won when serving either to the forehand or to the backhand. It turns out that professional players have approximately equal percentages of points won when mixing their targets.

It was also found that servers switched too often between forehand and backhand targets to be truly random. However, once a short-term "timing effect", where the returner will do better if she has returned a serve with the same stroke on the previous point, is accounted for, the mix becomes closer to random.

Others have also found that as points become more important, too many serves are directed to the backhand. This suggests that players could do better if they attacked the opponent's forehand return of serve more frequently at important moments. My hunch is that this shift to a more conservative serving strategy is related to "controlling one's destiny." By this I mean that, while equal percentages of points may be won by serving to either the forehand or the backhand at any moment in a match (if you have chosen the "optimal mix"), serving to the forehand carries with it the risk that the serve will be returned for a winner, i.e. a shot which you cannot touch. Under pressure, professional players

[7] Walker, M. and Wooters, J. "Minimax Play at Wimbledon." *American Economic Review* 91 (5):1521-1538 Dec 2001.

prefer to have another look at the ball by serving to the backhand, even if this means that more backhands will be returned into play.

> ***Rafael Nadal's serving strategy when playing Roger Federer offers a perfect example. He plays most, but not all, serves to Federer's weaker backhand and plays to his forehand far less frequently. However, he is not afraid to go to Federer's forehand and will even do so at important moments.***

By mixing his choices, Nadal is able to get the most out of his serve. This mixing of targets can also be applied to shot selection at any moment in a point. For example, when making an approach shot, most of the time, I will choose to attack an opponent's backhand, reserving my attacks on the forehand for relatively unimportant moments. At the highest levels of tennis even this choice must retain a small random component lest the opponent know what is coming.

In addition to the finding that pros are more predictable with their serving at key moments in a match, research also shows that professional players take less risk as points become more important. For example, rallies are longer in both men's and women's professional tennis during the more important points. This seems to contradict one of the Three Simple Rules of having a good game plan: DO NOT CHANGE A WINNING GAME.

The fact that rally length increases, i.e., professionals become more conservative with point importance suggests that the importance of a point also plays a crucial role in choosing the real world mix of shots and tactics. The Steady/Aggressive Lens allows us to understand that the only way that professionals would rationally alter their strategic decisions is if their "underlying abilities" changed as the points become more important. My contention, which I hope to prove in the next section, is that professionals change their games because they are doing a somewhat poor job of handling the increased stress at the key moments – their "underlying ability" to manage stress declines as importance rises. Hence, they become more conservative in their shot selection. In other words, pros need the 4-D System as much as lower-level players!

However, before looking at point importance, let's take a more detailed look at step 3 in the 4-D System: Relax or Calm Down. All of the top players know how to access this calm space. By doing so, the important moments seem like any other moment.

Chapter 5

Calm Down (3) – in detail

It is necessary to calm down physically between points in order to maintain your ability to execute your shots. Hitting your targets is easier when you are relaxed. If a point concludes with a well-executed relaxed stroke, you should give yourself positive reinforcement at this time to help stay in touch with the FEEL of a well-executed stroke. A simple "way to go, good relaxed stroke" is in order here. Conversely, if you over try or "muscle" a shot in an effort to get power, you must at this stage of 4-D immediately step back into relaxed mode. Match play can be stressful, and even the top pros "muscle" the ball at key moments. But they have the ability not to repeatedly make this same type of FEEL error. These types of errors are corrected during this stage (3) of the 4-D System.

Controlling your emotions is also a part of the calming-down stage between points. Better emotional control will enhance your ability to remain within the 4-D System. I am a big believer in "slow and steady wins the race." In order to achieve this, you must remain focused and calm. Controlling your breath is an effective way to maintain both physical and emotional control. Outwardly, with the rare exception of a Federer-like "come on!," you should exhibit minimal emotion. Inwardly however, you should be encouraging yourself whenever you have done something exceptionally well; and, conversely, admonishing yourself to remain disciplined whenever your execution or shot selection is lacking. Your ability to whip yourself into shape should be quick and sharp, but never taken personally, because the entire time you must recognize that you are playing a game! We have all witnessed athletes who pound their chests at the earliest signs of success only to see their short-lived euphoria turn to a flat despondence when things start to play out against them. I am not suggesting "no emotion"; however, maintaining emotional balance throughout a match is a critical element of creating the conditions for success.

All good doubles players know the value of supporting their partners with positive feedback immediately after they do something good. But very few players know that they should be using the same treatment on themselves. Don't give in to the negative emotions when you miss – instead make a correction and also look to encourage yourself when you do something well.

> ***One player at my club who is a really great guy had the following soliloquy the other day when we were playing doubles. He was my partner. I will call him Adam to protect his identity:***
>
> ***Adam (after missing a return of serve): "How bad is that? Well, I'll tell you, it's horrible, just horrible!"***
>
> ***Adam (after missing the next return of serve): "Will you wake up? Come on! How bad is that? You know what you need? Electro-shock, that's what you need! Electro-shock, that's it! ... (pause) But you know what? You're so bad even that won't help you!"***
>
> ***After the match, I saw Adam in the locker room with a towel draped over his head.***
>
> ***Adam: "My game is just so up and down. I can't explain it, but it's very frustrating"!***

Most of you probably don't react with anywhere near the intensity of Adam. But, to the extent that you do, it's quite clear that by going to an emotional place rather than the observer's place, you are wasting valuable time and energy between points and doing a poor job of preparing yourself for the upcoming point.

Relaxation, Point Importance and Performance

The Arousal/Performance chart below will help you to understand the relationship between relaxation, point importance, pressure, and performance. Performance means the ability to execute your shots. Below is a standard graph from sports psychology. From this graph, you can see that a player can access their best tennis when arousal levels are moderate. Higher levels of arousal diminish performance.

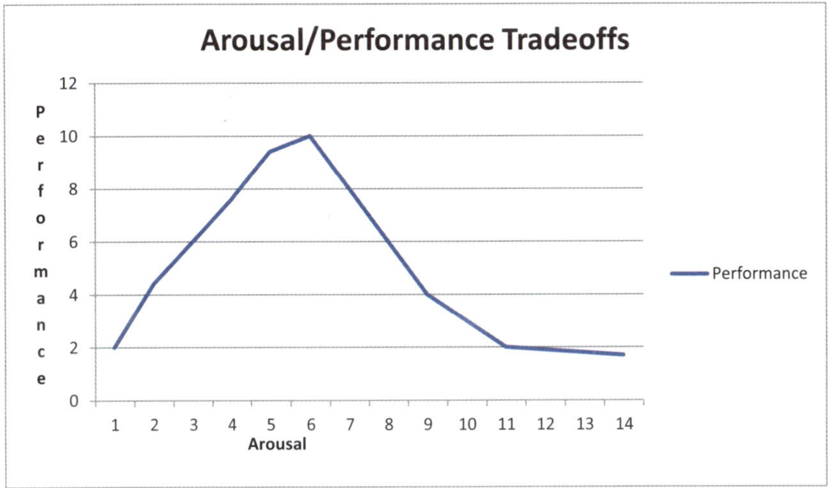

Stress or pressure, which is a part of any match, leads to arousal (a physiological response such as an increased heart rate) which leads to anxiety (the psychological component of the physiological response). So the direction of causation looks like this:

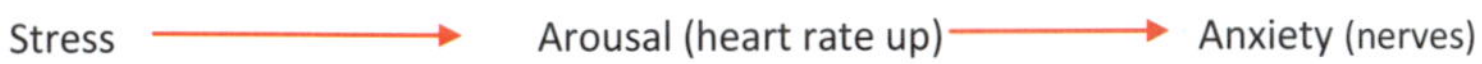

Research from sports psychology suggests that most individuals perform well below their peak levels when they are dealing with too much anxiety. Increased arousal, and therefore increased anxiety, is likely to manifest itself most when the points are more important. This is simply because more importance means more stress.

More importance → More stress

The Arousal/Performance graph demonstrates that most players play better when there is just enough, but not too much pressure on them. If pressure (arousal) is too low, performance will be subpar. As arousal increases, for example playing a practice match as opposed to a "fun" game, players will typically raise their levels. Or, you may think of the prototypical "practice player" who consistently performs better in practice than in a match. He wants to win in practice, but it's not as important as winning a match where arousal levels would take him to the right side of the graph where performance levels begin to drop off. In the graph, our typical player performs best (a 10) at arousal level 6. As his arousal level increases past 6, the performance of our typical player declines.

Simply "being in a match" is often sufficient to arouse most players to get near level 6. This is because they want to win – rarely will they be lackadaisical in a real match situation. However, as point importance increases, this increased importance usually brings arousal to levels which will diminish performance.

ONCE YOU UNDERSTAND THE RELATIVE IMPORTANCE OF POINTS WITHIN A GAME AND GAMES WITHIN A SET, YOU SHOULD BE ABLE TO SEE THAT IT IS BEST TO MAKE YOUR RISKIER PLAYS EARLIER IN A GAME/SET AND/OR WHEN THE SCORE IS LOPSIDED. TOGETHER, RELATIVELY LOW POINT IMPORTANCE AND SUFFICIENT AROUSAL BECAUSE YOU ARE PLAYING IN A MATCH MEANS THAT YOU HAVE A BETTER CHANCE OF EXECUTING YOUR RISKIER PLAYS AT THESE MOMENTS.

If you are able to execute your riskier play at moments of relatively low point importance, it will add to your confidence because success creates confidence. Confidence is clearly important to tennis players, yet it is almost always viewed as something that you either have or don't have.

The 4-D System suggests that a strong mental game includes the ability to "manufacture" confidence. YOU CAN USE THE SCORE TO BUILD YOUR CONFIDENCE WITHIN A MATCH.

Conversely, this also suggests that, if the point importance value is high, it is crucial for you to remind yourself to play at a less aroused level than the situation instinctively demands. Success on the more important points is strongly linked to your ability to manage your own tension level, both emotionally and physically. Or, to say this somewhat differently: higher point importance values will likely lead to a decline in the level of play of your opponent because she will become (and remain) too excited. If you can control your arousal to near optimal levels, you can continue to play the game which got you into a potentially winning position.

> ***I almost never call the score when I'm in a match EXCEPT when the opponent is on the verge of winning in a close match. In this way, I "remind" them of the importance of the point and thereby encourage them to play with too much tension.***

THIS MEANS THAT A KEY TO WINNING THE IMPORTANT POINTS IS TO PLAY THE SAME AND LET THE DECLINE IN YOUR OPPONENT'S LEVEL WIN THE POINT.

This concept is at odds with the all too familiar idea of "rising to the occasion." A player should, in nearly every situation, reject the idea that he needs to play better than "well" in order to win. Mats Wilander, multiple Grand-Slam champion, was a believer in this concept. When asked how he could repeatedly hit winning passing shots at the most crucial moments of a match, he responded: "I hit the ball as if it's just a regular shot."

In their recently published book, Analyzing Wimbledon[8] (2014), authors Franc Klaassen and Jan Magnus substantiate my thesis surrounding point importance and performance with data from four years of play (1992-1995). Ignoring the fact that the game of tennis has changed tactics/strategy since that time, their careful statistical analysis shows that "*Top players do not perform better, but lower-ranked players perform worse at important points*." Furthermore, they show that momentum or what they call a "winning mood" does not affect the performance of the top players, i.e., they play each point as if it were an island unto itself. For lower-ranked players, winning the previous point makes it somewhat more likely that they will win the next point. However, losing

---

[8] See pages 173-175 for details.

a point also makes it more likely that lower-ranked players will lose the next point. His data supports a hypothesis that the better players are more stable, i.e., meaning mentally stable. This finding provides convincing support that the 4-D System or something very similar to it is a driving force behind success in tennis.

There is additional evidence to support the hypothesis that lower-ranked players play worse at important points.[9] One researcher finds that both professional-level men and women play less aggressively as points increase in importance. Both unforced errors (u) and winners (w) decrease during the most important quartile (top 25%) of points played. Further evidence for decreased aggressiveness comes from the fact that the average length of the points, as measured by the number of shots hit during a point, increases. This is because the players are taking less risk. While this may be seen as a rational response to increased pressure, it also suggests that the decline in an opponent's play will most likely be the result of her "pushing" at crucial moments.

Professionals change to a more conservative strategy when the pressure rises. However, if their between-point ritual (the 4-D System!) were strong, they would be nearly immune to this change. Interestingly, pros are violating one of the basic tenets of tennis strategy: DO NOT CHANGE A WINNING GAME. This gear change is a clear violation of sticking with a winning plan. How should players go about improving their reactions to increased pressure?

IMPROVING YOUR ABILITY TO MANAGE TENSION LEVELS BETWEEN POINTS IS ENOUGH, IN AND OF ITSELF, TO RAISE YOUR GAME TO THE DEGREE NECESSARY TO CHANGE A 50/50 MATCH TO A 70/30 MATCH!

What would be the result if players maintained the same level of aggressiveness no matter what the score (level of point importance)? Research shows that if players were to play at the same level of aggressiveness which they do on the least important 75% of points, their probability of winning a 50/50 match increases to somewhere between 73 and 80%! This winning match

[9] M. Daniele Paserman, 'Gender Differences in Performance in Competitive Environments: Field Evidence from Professional Tennis Players', January 2010.

percentage (73-80%) is nearly exactly equivalent to the 70% winning percentage which would result from a 2% improvement in the percentage of points won. These results suggest that if a player could learn to inoculate himself against the demons of pressure, she would be far better off. The 4-D System does just that by having you touch base with your emotional and physical tension levels between points. Once you learn the system, this becomes easier and easier to do.

From the perspective of the 4-D System, excessive tension will cause a decline in performance for 2 reasons: 1) excessive tension will cause decreased racquet speed which causes players to play in an incorrect gear; this will lower performance; and 2) as stress causes a narrowing of focus, strategic choices become compromised. As we have seen, research has shown that servers do a somewhat poorer job of choosing serving targets at the most important moments in a match.

Klaassen and Magnus find that while momentum is statistically significant (not to be confused with meaningful!), it does NOT explain anything for the top players. This suggests a "mental stability" which transcends the emotional ups and downs of winning or losing the previous point. They also find that the top players play the same at important moments while lower-ranked opponents play worse.

As we have seen, professional tennis players of both genders do play more conservatively at the important moments. In another paper, Klaassen and Magnus find that players get more first serves in and hit fewer aces at break point, for example. And, as noted above, research shows that the length of the rally increases for both men and women at important moments in a match. What exactly are the important moments in a match? Can Point Importance be quantified?

Point Importance

Take the following exchange between a veteran baseball scout (Grady) and his numbers driven manager (Billy) from the movie *Moneyball*:

GRADY

This isn't how you put a team together. Scouting's about experience and baseball intuition.

BILLY

There's no such thing as intuition, just facts ...

Grady, you don't have special powers. You don't have the ability to look at a guy and "just know" because you're a scout with special powers. Your gut makes mistakes and makes them all of the time ... It's mythology. It doesn't have anything to do with "heart" or "wanting it" or romance of any kind. We're shopping in a new store – full of statistical analysis and equations and I get it that it all makes you feel useless but ...[10]

Despite the admonition "play every point", players who understand the game of tennis know that all points are not of equal value. In the Introduction, I mentioned the obvious difference between the value of the 0-0, 0-40 point and the value of a point at 5-all and deuce. These differences may actually be quantified using a concept called the "Importance of the Point."[11] The importance of a point is equal to the probability of winning a match given that a player wins that point minus the probability of winning the match given that he loses the point. The actual numerical values are not important. However, these values do

[10] Excerpt from the movie *Moneyball*.

[11] This definition of 'importance of the point' is taken from Klaassen, Franc J.G.M. and Magnus, Jan R. 'Are Points in Tennis Independent and Identically Distributed? Evidence from a Dynamic Binary Panel Data Model', *Journal of the American Statistical Association*, 96(454), June 2001, pp. 500-509. In math talk, Importance of a Point = Probability{Win match|win point} – Probability{Win match|lose point}.

serve the purpose of illustrating the *relative* importance of points at different scores. You should familiarize yourself with the *relative* values of points so you are able to make a near instantaneous assessment of their importance. As I explain below, this will be invaluable in helping you to set the correct level of risk-taking – the correct balance between aggression and patience.

Critics of point importance often make their case with reasoning similar to the following (from the blog of Happy Bhalla, well-known tennis pro and big-point detractor):

Brad Gilbert defines a big point as any point that can win a game or any point that if won would lead to a game- winning point. This logic is untenable. Imagine a four-rung ladder, from which an apple can be plucked from a tree. The object is to pluck the apple. From the fourth rung one can reach the apple, but unless one climbs the third rung they will not reach the fourth rung; similarly the third rung cannot be reached until one has already arrived at the second and so forth. This metaphor illustrates that climbing each rung is equally important, because one leads to the next. At the very least, we would have to call each point big.

Bhalla is correct: Gilbert's logic *is* untenable. As you will see, the *relative* importance of points can be measured. But Bhalla's analogy is untenable as well. In tennis, it's not just about getting the apple – it's about getting the apple while the opponent is also scaling his own ladder and trying to get the apple first. It is your *relative* position which matters! Once you understand this, it will change the way that you play the game.

I will demonstrate that the value of a point is highest in the 3rd (deciding) set and becomes higher as a set or game increases in length as long as the score remains close.

For example, points are more important at 30-all than at 40-0 or love-40. Points are also more important at 4-all than they are at 5-1. And points are more important at one set all than they are in the first or second set. This will all be spelled out in detail in

the sections which follow. And it's also fairly obvious! However, what may be new to you is the RELATIVE value of the points!

An Even (50/50) match

To keep things simple at the start, in order to increase your understanding of how to use the score, let's assume a match between you and an equally-matched opponent. Just like the tossing of a fair coin, the probability of either of you winning a point, winning a game, winning a set, or winning the match is 50/50. For a tennis match to be competitive, the probabilities that either player could win any given point must be very close. For example, even if the split is 55/45, which at first glance doesn't seem to be a large difference, the probability of the better player winning the match is 91%.

In the Tables which illustrate my examples, the lowest point values will be colored in dark blue. As the value of the point increases, the color will change to light blue, then green, then orange, and finally, the most important points, in red.

Table 1[12]

The Importance of Points within a Game: 50/50 Match

50%	**Importance of point in game**			
	0	15	30	40
0	.313	.313	.250	.125
15	.313	.375	.375	.250
30	.250	.375	.500	.500
40	.125	.250	.500	.500

[12] A special thanks to Prof Brian Rogers of Northwestern University for providing me with the spreadsheets from his paper 'Performing Best When It Matters Most: Evidence From Professional Tennis' co-written by Julio Gonzalez-Diaz, Olivier Gossner and Brian W. Rogers, *Journal of Economic Behavior and Organization,* 2012, **84**, (3), p. 767-781 which make the calculations in this chapter easily accessible.

Let's look at the importance of points at various scores within a game, leaving the game and set score out of the picture for now. Two things are readily apparent from the values in Table 1. First, values are higher when the score is close or even – compare the 40-15 and 15-40 points with the 0-0, 15-all, 30-all, and deuce points. And secondly, values are higher at the end of a game – compare 0-0 and 15-all with the 30-all and deuce points. It should come as no surprise that points at 30-all, 40-30 or 30-40, and deuce have the most importance.

It is crucial that you see that the points at 0-40 and 40-0 have only ¼ the value of the (red) most important points – remember, it is the *relative* values which matter. What does this mean for the competitive player? It suggests for BOTH the server and the receiver that a higher risk point should be played at these extremes in the score. Keep in mind that playing a higher risk point does NOT mean that you are no longer giving your best effort to win the point. It simply means that you are going beyond your comfort zone to "make something happen" sooner rather than later. An alternative, but nearly equivalent way of saying this is that players should run something other than their highest percentage tennis play when in a lop-sided scoring situation. Here are two concrete examples, one from singles and one from doubles.

Imagine a singles match on a very hot day against an excellent retriever. You are serving at 40-0. You have faulted your first serve and decide to spin the ball in on your second serve. Now is NOT the time to play a long grueling point which might tire you out for the rest of the game or the next game as well. Now is the time to go for your forehand or play a delicate drop right at the start of the point. If you make it, you have the game and you have some additional confidence along with all of your energy. If you miss it, you still have a 40-15 lead, i.e., two more chances to close out the game. Here the relative "importance of the point" helps you to choose the right type of point to play -- in this case, a short point.

Now, imagine a doubles match where the opposition is serving at 40-0. Her serve is fairly good, but not overpowering. You have been returning solid basic cross- court returns up until this point in the match (even if it was just one prior point, i.e., this is the first receiving game of the match). This is an excellent time to take a forehand return and go after the net player. If you make it, you've boosted your confidence and put a bit of fear into your opposition at a time in the match where the point was not worth very much anyway. If you miss, you really have not lost anything.

Most people who read about the risk implications of the lop-sided score have no difficulty understanding the concept when it comes to the 40-0 lead. However, when they are trailing 0-40, most players will hesitate to take a chance. This is a misunderstanding of point importance. When trailing 0-40, you should hope to play a successful higher-risk point. The hope is that this success will "rattle" your opponent sufficiently on the next couple of points and enable you to make a comeback in the game. After all, at 0-40, the probability of coming back from playing your usual game in a 50/50 match is less than 7%.

The Importance of the Game within the Set: 50/50 Match

Table 2

Importance of the game

I \ II	0	1	2	3	4	5
0	.246	.246	.219	.164	.094	.031
1	.246	.273	.273	.234	.156	.063
2	.219	.273	.313	.313	.250	.125
3	.164	.234	.313	.375	.375	.250
4	.094	.156	.250	.375	.500	.500
5	.031	.063	.125	.250	.500	.500

Above is Table 2 for Importance of the Game within a set for two evenly matched (50/50) players. The colors signifying the relative importance are the same as the ones which I used to illustrate the importance of points within a game in Table 1.

The "Importance of a Game" is defined as the difference in the probability of winning a set conditional upon whether or not you win or lose the game in question.[13]

There are two important things to note from this Table. First, the values at 3 games or below for either player are less than the values at the end of the set: 4-all, 4-5 or 5-4, or 5-all. How would you use this to become a more effective player? Recall that using a mixed strategy is optimal. Bjorn Borg was a master at using the early stages of a match to gather information on his opponent and use this information in the later more important stages of a set to win. He would mix things up when it didn't matter too much and then zero in on his best plan when it was closing time.

Just as with the point score, when the game scores are fairly close, the importance is relatively higher. Conversely, lopsided scores like 0-3, 0-4, 0-5, 1-4, and 1-5 have significantly lower values. The game importance at 5-all is about 16 times higher than that at 0-5. This large disparity is the result of the fact that the outcome of the set has been almost certainly determined at 5-0 or 0-5. However, it also means that, just as with the 40-0 and 0-40 examples above, the *relative importance* is extremely low. This means that both the player leading in the score and the player trailing in the score have an opportunity to increase their risk-taking and be successful because stress levels will be comparatively low. Failure to understand this can have dire consequences for closing out a match.

One of my students told me of a doubles match where the other team raced to a 5-1 lead. She said: "we realized all of the pressure was on them (to close out the set), so we relaxed, got more aggressive and won the set 7-5." The team with the lead failed to realize that they too should have been playing more aggressively. Remember, a 5-1 lead means that you should be marginally raising the risk-taking in your play.

[13] Importance of a Game = Prob{win set | win game} – Prob{win set | lose game}.

The game score within a set can also play an important secondary role in shot selection. Here is an example of using score importance as the relevant concept when deciding where to attack with an approach shot. Here the importance of the game within the set is the key.

As a singles player in my prime, my game relied on getting to the net and finishing or forcing errors with my volley. As a patient baseliner who waited for my chance to come in, I would focus my attack on my opponent's backhand, but would also, particularly during the early moments in a match (before someone got to four games), direct a few approaches to my opponent's forehand side as well. This was all based upon the idea that if he knew what was coming for certain, his defense would be that much better at the end of the set. As the "Importance of the Game" Table 2 illustrates, I was keeping him honest when the game values were lower and setting him up for running the play that I wanted when the game values were higher.

Therefore, the importance of a point or a game can change the way in which you plan to play. And the reality of the differences in importance also requires that you transition to step #3 of the 4-D System: Calm Down. To the extent that you become more adept at calming down, important points become more like relatively unimportant ones. This is what the findings of Klaassen and Magnus tell us: the top players play the same at the important moments.

If the game score is in your favor, it is an important skill to know how to ratchet up your attack by a small, but still meaningful amount. Most big leads which you will garner are the result of your opponent making too many unforced errors. Ultimately, most good players refuse to lose by making errors, so at some point you can expect them to go into "solid" mode. The tennis expression for this is to Refuse to Lose.

For example, in doubles this might mean that your opponent eschews low percentage returns and elects to play cross court drives. This is a perfect time to increase your poaching, putting the squeeze on them.

In the 2012 US Open, Marin Cilic led Andy Murray in their round of 16 match by a set and 4-0. Murray immediately raised his risk level by attacking second serves and playing otherwise more aggressively. This was the correct response to the score. Cilic, on the other hand, began to play "not to lose." He allowed Murray to control the type of points being played and he ultimately lost the set in a tiebreaker. The next two sets were easy for Murray: 6-1, 6-1. Because Cilic did not appear to understand the freedom which was his with the second set 4-0 lead, he squandered an opportunity for perhaps the best win of his career at that time. He should have raised his own risk level to match Murray's.

Playing to the score is a subtle part of match management. Your basic game plan is set by the Steady/Aggressive paradigm. Then the 4-D System will have you check in with the score before the start of each point. This check-in may have you adjust the desired risk level and gear for the point about to begin. Once this is set, the score is FORGOTTEN.

This bears repeating: THE SOLE PURPOSE OF CHECKING IN WITH THE SCORE IS TO HELP YOU TO SET THE CORRECT LEVEL OF RISK WITH WHICH TO PLAY THE NEXT POINT. ONCE YOU SET THE RISK LEVEL, YOU MUST FORGET THE SCORE!

Thoughts while the ball is in play such as "I have to get this point!" or "You have to win this!" are counter-productive and will only hinder performance. The 4-D System will help you to eliminate this type of thinking from your mental game by resetting your focus to "see the ball into the strings" before each and every point.

If you are trailing by a large margin, this can also help you to mount a possible comeback. At this moment, by recognizing the importance of a game in lop-sided situations, you should recognize that you will almost certainly lose. The acknowledgement of imminent defeat lowers the pressure that you feel and sets the stage for a possible comeback. If you look back to the Arousal/Performance graph, this brings you down from higher arousal levels closer to the optimal, level 6. Acknowledgement of nearly certain defeat does NOT mean giving up or anything close to it. What it does mean is the recognition that there is less pressure, and with it, an opportunity to play better and therefore change the type of points being played.

> ***In a recent mixed doubles match, my partner and I trailed 3-6, 1-4, 30-40. My usual attacking game was resulting in too many unforced errors. Initially, I accepted this as merely a bad streak in what would become a victory characterized by my dominating play. However, as we reached the endgame, I realized that I was doing a poor job of controlling my tension level and adjusted the gear on my strokes down by one level. By doing so, I changed the type of point being played. Our opponents, accustomed to getting unforced errors, could not adjust, and we came back to win in a super tiebreak.***

The importance of a point can often cause a player to rush either through the Adjust/Plan phase (2) of the 4-D System or get stuck thinking about the score.

> ***We all know the partners, who at important moments in doubles, turn to you and say: "get this point." Or, who say at 15-40: "only two to deuce." "Like duh? You don't think that I can even keep score"? I think to myself.***
>
> ***Another example is a returner in singles who has been successful at playing 3rd -and 4th-gear rallies against a server. He is winning enough of these points that he is getting break opportunities. However, at break point and wanting to win that***

next point very badly, he slows his game to 2nd gear. The server controls him at this slower gear each time and ultimately holds his serve. Here the returner was either not adequately aware of the gear which gave him his opportunities or was doing a poor job of going to the next step, Calming Down. This makes it impossible for him to play the right type of point to close out the game.

As noted above, professional players are not immune to this tendency to back off at crucial moments in a match. This means that players of all levels need to seek improvement in their tension management which will improve their gear management. Understanding both point and game importance will help you to set the correct level of risk as well as to suggest *when* to mix in your slightly lower percentage plays.

Point Importance – Is There More Proof?

We've seen that lower-ranked professional players performed less well at the more important moments. Their probability of winning an important point declined.

Clearly, the response to point importance varies by level of player, but does it really explain a tennis player's success? Using data from 12 years of the US Open, researchers have demonstrated that "critical abilities" (their term for performing well on important points) are a key determinant of success on the pro tour.[14]

Here they measure success not as winning a point but as having an effect on a player's ranking over his career. They are able to measure this effect after taking account of players' relative serving and returning skills. The correlation of "critical ability" with a player's ranking is nearly equivalent to returning ability as a measure of player success. From this we can conclude that the ability to respond to pressure is a skill and that the rewards to this skill are substantial.

[14] "Performing Best When It Matters Most: Evidence From Professional Tennis" co-written by Julio Gonzalez-Diaz, Olivier Gossner and Brian W. Rogers, *Journal of Economic Behavior and Organization,* 2012, **84**, (3), p. 767-781.

Players of all levels can benefit from developing the mental skills necessary to play well at the important moments. The mental skills which you will develop by using the 4-D System will almost certainly make you a better player when the pressure is on.

Now, you will make the final transition: from Calming Down to Watching the Ball.

"There are three stages: Thoughtless being. Thought. Return to thoughtless being. Do not confuse the first and third stages. Thoughtless being is attained by everyone, the return to thoughtless being by a very few."[15]

Chapter 6

Watch the Ball (4) – in detail

This is the final switch in focus and it occurs just before the point is about to begin. Immediately before the start of each point you should remind yourself to look the ball into the strings. If you can execute this, FEEL is accessed, and you can fairly reliably hit your targets. Along with wallowing in negative emotion or excessive focus on the importance of a point, this failure to check in with this simple instruction immediately before the start of each point explains most of the errors in tennis.

The complete 4-D System is now in place. A player should, observe what just happened (1), check in with his game plan and the score, and choose his target and gear (2), get his body and emotions into a relaxed and centered place (3), and remind himself to see the contact (4). He must stay in sequence from the end of one point until the start of the next point.

For many players, the time at contact is all too rushed, much like the childhood game of "hot potato." In practice, players should deliberately exaggerate the amount of time which they spend visually at contact. This exaggeration of "patience within the shot" will help a player to know what it is to look the ball into the strings.

FEEL – The Ability to Hit Targets[16]

You all know those days when you "have the FEEL" on the tennis court. Shots seem to flow magically to good targets and all of those shots which are close to the line are going in. For most players, particularly club players, accessing FEEL is a rather random event, something analogous to winning a few dollars in

[15] The Art of Fielding, by Chad Harbach, p.16. My book is about making you, the reader, one of the very few.
[16] Adapted from "Feel in Tennis" by Bob Schewior, *Tennis Week*, Feb. 7, 1980, p.11.

the Mega Millions lottery. This chapter will not only describe the various components of FEEL, but will help you to develop a systematic approach to gaining access to your FEEL with a detailed description of how to warm up. Imagine you can bottle those good FEEL days and bring them with you to the court nearly every time!

The quotation which begins this chapter captures the mental quiet which is a key component of delivering the ball to the intended target (FEEL). Once the ball is in play, you need to focus ONLY on seeing the blur of the racquet as it strikes the ball. Incredibly, all other thoughts, such as "down-the-line" or "cross court" while the ball is in play will be detrimental to your performance. This is what is meant by the "return to thoughtless being"!

FEEL is the process through which top players deliver the ball to their intended targets. To the extent that club players of all levels can imitate the top pros in their approach to the game, they will also begin to hit their targets more consistently. FEEL is best understood when it is broken down into three parts:

(1) A player's ability to observe the ball being hit by the strings.

To illustrate the observing contact component (1) of FEEL, a valuable aid is the instruction to "keep your head still." Strictly speaking, the human eye is not quick enough actually to see the ball hit the strings, but you should play each and every shot *as if* you could. What you can see is the "blur" of the racquet as it passes through the contact zone. If there is any doubt about this, the Youtube videos of Roger Federer's forehand in slow motion should provide convincing evidence.

> ***One satellite player that I knew had an interesting way of using his eyes during the warm-up. He would keep his head still at contact and move his eyes to look at the court/wall next to him before looking on the opposite side of the net. Implicitly, playing with FEEL means having trust in one's shots and abilities because a player is not "peeking" to see where***

the opponent is. FEEL is the implementation of the old cliche': play the ball and don't play the opponent.

A longtime friend and tennis colleague, Chris Busa, uses an alternative phrase, "after image", to describe what I mean by seeing the blur. In some ways, this is a more accurate concept because not all shots have sufficient racquet speed to make a blur. For example, the "after image" of a volley is a racquet frozen at contact while simultaneously witnessing the blur streak of the ball leaving the strings.

(2) Sensing the tension levels in key parts of your body.

Optimal tension levels depend upon the shot being executed. For example, small differences in grip tension determine whether or not a defensive lob is well executed or not – too tight a grip and the ball flies long; too loose of a grip and the lob lands short. Similarly, a player's back muscles must be tightened on high volleys, but relaxed when attacking a groundstroke with no pace.

Each of the different strokes requires its own grip tension. As a general rule, the longer the stroke, the more relaxed is the grip on the racquet.

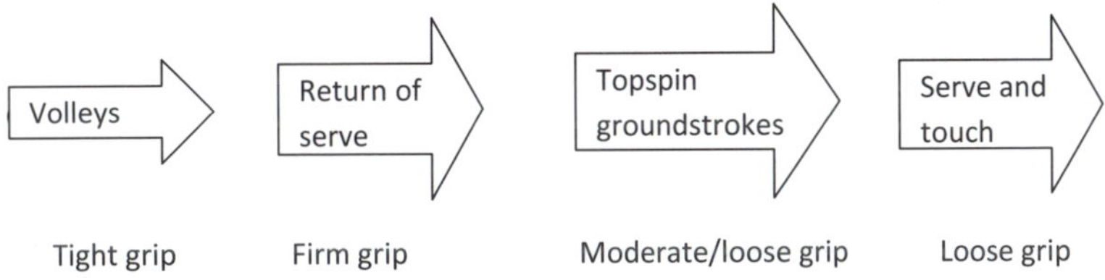

A simple progression from a tighter to a looser grip is shown above. The volley is a timing shot which requires a very firm squeeze of the grip just as you see the ball hit the strings. If the opponent has a very strong serve, then the return must be hit with a shorter blocking motion with the grip firmness somewhere between a volley and a groundstroke. Topspin groundstrokes, particularly when wanting to add pace or absorb power are hit with a more relaxed grip. And finally, serves and the entire family of touch shots (drop shots, drop volleys, lobs) are hit with a very relaxed grip.

Most players run into problems with their FEEL because they are squeezing the racquet too tightly on nearly all of their shots. In part, this is due to the fact that they have learned in other areas of life, that more effort typically yields better results. In tennis, and many other sports, less is more. For most tennis players trying harder when executing their strokes is counter-productive. Access to FEEL means less brute force.

However, as a player you must be careful to differentiate: less trying does not mean less focus. Often players will send a ball flying accompanied by a loud exclamation "too much"; I always counter "not enough" – not enough focus. In other words, these players lost their focus on seeing the ball into the strings.

Your ability to be able to vary your grip tension is therefore an essential part of being able to get the ball to your target. But being aware of the tension in other parts of the body is crucial as well.

For example, as noted in the example above, on a high volley the back muscles and core must contract to form solid support for the shot. This same contraction would be counter-productive on both the serve and overhead where the looser preparation and swing are needed.

3) Sensing one's target area without letting that awareness interfere with points (1) and (2).

The target component of FEEL (3) may be demonstrated with a very simple exercise. Players should pair off across the net at the service line. One player, the tosser, will look at the catcher (the target) and then close her eyes and throw the ball directly to the catcher so that the catcher receives the ball on a fly. Players are immediately surprised at the accuracy of their tosses. You should toss the ball over the head of, or on one bounce to, the catcher – again, with your eyes closed. This is the essence of FEEL – sensing your body tension and the target without looking at the target.

It is a useful clue when developing FEEL to use the top of the net as a reference point when making your shots. Correcting errors becomes as simple as "aim higher" or "aim lower."

Simultaneous execution of all three elements enables a player to FEEL a particular shot.

As I mentioned above, FEEL can be learned. When first attempting to get the focus required to see the ball into the strings, some players may feel lost. Players who are used to peeking at their targets can have a difficult time making the adjustment to look the ball into the strings. To make this learning process easier, teachers should use "dead ball feeds" meaning that the fed ball is not returned. This solves the problem of the student worrying too much about what the opponent is going to do with the ball.

In Tennis Science (2015), authors Reid, et al. provide an excellent pictorial on "gaze behavior," their term for how your eyes should work when playing tennis. They suggest that players on the men's tour use the complete "head still" approach which I advocate for developing FEEL. The women's tour, they suggest, is characterized by "partial fixation" where the player's head moves immediately after impact.

Recall from our discussion of point importance that there was a gender difference in the ratio of unforced errors to winners for women in the top 25% of points ordered by importance. I submit that "total" versus "partial" fixation is the most likely explanation for this increase in unforced errors. A moving head is a technical error and technical weaknesses often don't show up until the pressure is on.

Like Tim Gallwey (The Inner Game of Tennis, 1974), I believe in the general concept of the two Selves: Self 1, the conscious teller, and Self 2, the automatic doer. Gallwey's key insight was that the conscious mind most often interferes with what Self 2 knows (Self 2 knows how to get the ball to the target). This is what makes gaining access to Self 2 a doable, yet still difficult task. The 4-D System makes it possible to use both the insights of Self 1 and the let-it-happen aspect of Self 2. Do not misunderstand me -- Self 1 is a major contributor to success in competitive tennis. There would be no great players without Self 1. Without Self 1's analysis there would be no "game plans" or the ability to identify and pick on an opponent's weaknesses. The secret, as I hope to demonstrate, is to keep Self 1 quiet while the ball is in play so that Self 2 can do his thing. This is the meaning of the quotation from The Art of Fielding at the start of this chapter.

It is crucial to understand that the groundwork for FEEL is laid before a player comes on the court. As Tim Gallwey notes in The Inner Game of Tennis, focusing on one's breathing is a simple and effective way to become more relaxed. In particular, a long inhale through the nose followed by a long exhale through the mouth can have an immediate relaxing effect when repeated three times.

Personally, I have found the techniques of self-hypnosis to be even more effective. Essentially these techniques involve tensing and relaxing various parts of the body in turn (the toes, the feet, the calves, the thighs, etc.) so that you become acutely aware of the differences between the tension levels. At the end of the preparation, you will be completely in touch with the differences between a relaxed and a tense way of going. This will enable you to access the relaxed way much more easily.

Playing with FEEL has an important consequence for target selection and point construction – you should be playing for The Forced Error.

What is FEEL?

The Three Elements of Feel
Eyes at contact point
"See the blur"
Tension feedback from grip and entire body
Awareness of the target

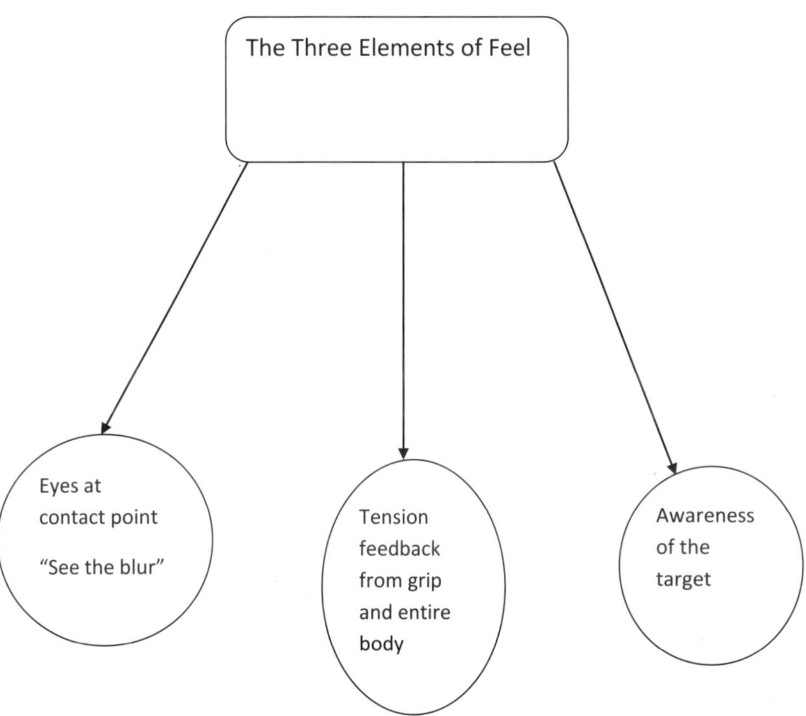

The Forced Error

All competitive players understand that unforced errors are the bane of a tennis player's existence: good competitors refuse to beat themselves. However, these players also recognize that merely getting the ball back one more time will not be successful, particularly as the level of play rises. At the same time, players soon learn that going for winners rarely pays off, but usually results in their own unforced error. A key idea behind using FEEL to execute a well-designed game plan is to play for the FORCED ERROR. A FORCED ERROR is an error caused by the quality of either your own or your opponent's shot. Typically the shot causing a FORCED ERROR is good enough to compromise an opponent's balance without the risk of hitting right near the lines.

With the concept of FEEL, a player learns to "play from within." This means that, at the moment of impact, the relationship of utmost importance is between you and the ball, i.e., seeing the ball into contact. As soon as you begin to go for winners, the relationship which dominates becomes one between you and your opponent.

Once, when checking in for a tournament, the director informed me that "your opponent is not yet here." "Yes he is," I responded, referring to myself.

Essentially, "playing from within" means that, with the exception of some shots which are just so easy that they can be hit for winners, all shots are played so that it is ok with you if the opponent touches the ball! The key for you is to sense the threshold between the reaching of the ball either with or without balance on the part of your opponent. Once your opponent is off balance, his ability to hit targets forcefully and accurately is compromised. Once you understand and accept this idea, nearly all of the unforced errors which result from going for winners will evaporate from your game.

The best players control the ball through FEEL, i.e. with their bodies. A winner is, by definition, a shot that an opponent cannot touch. When you instruct your body to "hit the ball so that it cannot be touched", your body will listen. Each over-hit "out" ball as well as those which slam into the net is following this instruction to keep the ball away from the opponent. Incredibly, this means that, many times when you miss a shot, your body is simply doing what you asked it to do! If you can reprogram the instructions, the errors will evaporate! This reprogramming of the target through the concept of The Forced Error is an important component of game plan formulation because it reduces unforced errors while, at the same time, pressuring an opponent.

> ***I shared this insight on forced errors with a top female singles player at the club. However, when she went to implement the concept, she said that she repeatedly was telling herself "don't hit a winner." There are two things to note here: 1) I never said "don't hit a winner." But I did say that winners should be thought of as well struck shots – not "going for a winner"; and 2) people in general do not respond well to being told what they should NOT do. Positive instructions, i.e., "here's what I want to do" are far more helpful.***

This is also true for world-class pros. Each of the Grand Slams provides data for every match. Categories include unforced errors, winners (including service), serving percentage, etc. But, if I am correct that the FORCED ERROR usually tells an important part of the story about a match, these statistics are like reading a Sherlock Holmes detective story without Sherlock in the plot (Ok, without Watson in the plot!). In each of the seven matches played from the quarterfinals until the finals at Roland Garros and the US Open in 2012, the player with fewer unforced errors won the match! However, the FORCED ERROR category was a slightly better predictor than winners in determining the victor.

To reiterate: A forcing shot is a shot played with enough pace, spin, and direction such that the opponent is able to get his racquet on the ball, but is unable, in most cases, to control his stroke to a precise target. The result of a forcing shot will either be a forced error or a weaker reply. If the FORCED ERROR is the key to success, this suggests that all players who are trying to improve must develop at least one, and possibly several, weapons. Suffice it to say that players must be able to play consistently "aggressively enough" to utilize the FORCED ERROR framework. This requires both solid fundamentals and being well acquainted with their 3rd and 4th gears.

> ***One of the commentators on the TennisChannel has coined the phrase "big shots to big targets." This stands for hitting 4th gear shots repeatedly, but NOT near the lines. This is an alternative to playing 3rd gear shots with finer targets. Either of these concepts will help you to improve in baseline rallies.***

> ***Warning: mental training can do a lot, but it cannot solve all problems! Again, I will give you an example from the 4.0/4.5 women's singles program. One of the players has an exceptional backhand and a very dodgy forehand. The forehand repeatedly breaks down under pressure. She attributes this to nerves and insists that she just needs to play more and things will work out. My assessment is that there is a significant technical flaw in the stroke and all of the playing in the world will not do much to change that. Sometimes improvement means making a BIG CHANGE.***

Without this acquaintance, a player cannot force errors, and without this capability he cannot win matches against higher quality opponents. Frequently, players practice in 3rd gear but play matches in 1st or 2nd gear which gives the opponent too much time to get into good hitting position. The opponent is able to capitalize on the slower pace and seize the initiative. When asked to play more aggressively, these same players go immediately to 5th gear and make too many errors. Gear management is a crucial part of what happens between points and it is highly correlated with a player's ability to manage tension/arousal levels.

Because most points at the better levels of tennis are played in 3rd gear (neutral), another source of the 2% improvement that you should be looking for is to improve the depth, spin, and pace on your neutral shots. This will force your opponent to take risks when she really doesn't want to.

The concepts of Court Geometry, Percentage Tennis, and the role of The Forced Error must all be running in the background of a your mind much like a virus checking program on a computer. There is no need to check in with these concepts between each point. However, if a glaring violation occurs, such as going for a groundstroke winner from 5 feet behind the baseline, the understanding implicit in these concepts immediately becomes conscious and prevents you from continuing with this self-defeating shot selection.

Against younger stronger opponents, I often find myself going for aggressive down the line shots too early in the rally because I know that often I will be outrun if I play longer points. However, I also know that I need to play with better court geometry on my side. Understanding court geometry makes me play a tougher level of tennis – even if I don't win! ☹

At the lower levels of competitive tennis, each of these components of a solid understanding of tennis needs to be taught and continually reinforced with game situation drills. At the higher levels of tennis, these concepts have been internalized and a player is ready to develop a game plan based upon her assessment of both her and her opponent's strengths and weaknesses.

The Warm-up

The warm-up is the crucial time for accessing FEEL. After all, it is unlikely that FEEL will magically appear in the middle of a match which you have begun without it. I find mini-tennis ideal for accomplishing this. Here is the step-by-step check-in procedure which I use in the warm-up:

1) Consciously relax. The tension control exercises have prepared me to be able to implement this.

2) Look for the blur on each groundstroke as the racquet passes through contact implementing Gallwey's "bounce-hit" where a player calls

"bounce" to himself as the ball bounces and "hit" as he sees it the racquet.

3) Finish each stroke gradually increasing racquet speed. There should be no pushing or bunting of the ball in the warm-up.

4) Increase awareness of striking the ball from the center of my body. Basically this means that I am checking in with my groundstroke technique.

I used the word access when first describing FEEL and it is crucially important here. It means that each time that you come to the court, you must prepare properly. Players who consistently arrive for practices/drills/matches 5-10 minutes late virtually guarantee their own failure. I have heard that Rafael Nadal, a man who values precision, actually warms up for varying amounts of time – he warms up for as long as it takes until he can FEEL the ball. There are no shortcuts, although it should be noted that, as you become more accomplished at arriving on court in the correct mental state, the time required to get to this place diminishes significantly.

Once on the court, none of the steps may be skipped. For example, if a player bunts the ball around in the warm-up all the while chatting about some superfluous subject with the person next to him/her, I can virtually guarantee that he will not FEEL. There is no focus on witnessing the blur, no centering of the shots in the core of the body, and no return to thoughtless being. Hence, there won't be any exceptional tennis being played.

This detailed warmup process is very much like the experience of doing yoga. As your mind gradually begins to pay attention to the things that matter, the encumbrances which prevent you from gaining access to FEEL gradually fall away. Once these meaningless distractions have been shed, it becomes possible to access FEEL, and with it, the magic of hitting your targets.

Maintaining FEEL in a Competitive Season

There is an extensive literature on periodisation, or how to find the right balance of training and competition so that you may peak at the desired moment. Generally, training is divided into four phases: Preparatory, Pre-competition, Competition, and Transition or Active Rest. The length and intensity of each of these phases differs depending upon one's level of play.

For the top professionals, this means peaking for the Grand Slams. For college and USTA players, this means peaking for their 2-3 month competitive seasons as well as any playoffs. It is my experience that many USTA players participate on multiple teams during the peak USTA season. Extended periods of intense competition may lead to problems such as burnout or overuse injuries. They may also make it impossible for players to make "adjustments" to their games because they are always looking to win. When you look to win, you stick with what you know best -- that is what you have been doing -- even if it hasn't been working.

Because match play produces more stress than training, many of these multiple-team players actually stagnate or become worse over the course of their 2-3 month intense competition phase. During this phase it is crucial that players who are looking to improve and sustain their high level of play maintain contact with their FEEL. This means relaxed hitting without playing points or keeping score. They should also make time for drilling a weakness which has been uncovered in the course of match play. This gives them at least some chance of making "adjustments" to their games in the middle of a competitive season.

Practicing to Improve

Because FEEL is so important in getting the ball to the target, paying attention to the correct things must be practiced all of the time when a player is trying to improve. However, it is also important for each and every one of you reading this book to understand that the relative level of your practice partners is also a critical component of improvement.

Nearly always, players want to "play up" while on their quests to improve. While this instinct is well-intended, it is often misplaced. There is a better way to look at the goal of improvement. It helps to look at tennis as simply two games: the first is offense (when you are dominating play); the second is defense (when you are getting pushed around). You can easily see that always "playing up" means that you are most likely playing defense nearly all of the time. This is true because the better player will have no trouble attacking your serve and you will be on the defensive immediately when faced with his serve. Your offensive skills will most likely go undeveloped. Therefore, it is crucial when you are trying to improve that you practice with players both above and below your level. As long as their abilities relative to your own are "close enough," you will benefit from such practices and be able to develop all aspects of your game.

In addition, confidence is a large intangible in tennis. Continuously practicing with players of higher ability and always competing against better players will end up denting the confidence of most players. Mixing the levels of your practice partners is an important part of staying on the road to improvement. The ITF suggests a win percentage of about 70% for aspiring juniors to build their confidence along with their games.

Summary

FEEL is absolutely critical if you are to develop your ability to hit targets in a reliable way. FEEL begins with a relaxed body and grip and requires that you focus *as if* you can see the ball hit the strings. Without developing your ability to keep your head still at the point of contact throughout a stroke, you are putting an effective lid on your ability to improve.

Developing FEEL is best practiced with "dead ball" feeds where your practice partner or coach is feeding you easily handled shots which are not returned. Gradually, the intensity of these shots should be ratcheted up to game speed. Once your ability to handle the "dead ball" feeds improves, you are ready to attempt to play with FEEL in real game situations.

Chapter 7

Point Importance – more detail

Table 3

Importance of point in 50/50 match

love-love	**0**	**15**	**30**	**40**
0	.038	.038	.031	.015
15	.038	.046	.046	.031
30	.031	.046	.062	.062
40	.015	.031	.062	.062

For those of you interested in getting an even more detailed look at Point Importance, Chapter 7 will fill in more information. If you feel fairly confident of your understanding, you should skip ahead to Chapter 8.

Table 3 highlights the importance of each point right at the start of a match. Notice that the importance values are far smaller than those in Table 1. This is because, taken in this larger context, the value of each individual point is lower: obviously any individual point has a far smaller impact on the outcome of the entire match than it does on the outcome of any single game. Table 3 provides a baseline from which you can compare values at the start of a match with those later in a match, including tiebreak values. It also provides a reference point to compare point importance when you and your opponent are not exactly evenly matched (50/50).

How to Play a Tiebreak

Let's look at Table 4 below for some clues as to how you should manage risk in a 12-point tiebreak. Everything that I say here will apply all the more to the popular Super-breaker (1st player to 10 win by 2) used in all USTA matches for rated players and at the professional level for many doubles matches simply because the Super-breaker is longer than the 12-pont tiebreak. The point importance values in the Table below reflect those for a tiebreak in the 3rd set of a match. This is the decider – it is as important as it can get. Once again, let's say that you and your opponent are exactly even: this is a 50/50 match.

Table 4

Tiebreak Point Importance: 50/50 Match

I \ II	0	1	2	3	4	5	6
0	**.226**	.226	.205	.164	.109	.055	.016
1	.226	**.246**	.246	.219	.164	.094	.031
2	.205	.246	**.273**	.273	.234	.156	.063
3	.164	.219	.273	**.313**	.313	.250	.125
4	.109	.164	.234	.313	**.375**	.375	.250
5	.055	.094	.156	.250	.375	**.500**	.500
6	.016	.031	.063	.125	.250	.500	**.500**

The first thing to recognize here is that, just as in a regular game, the importance of the point increases dramatically as players approach the end of the tiebreak. And, as in the standard tennis game, when the score is even (those points highlighted in **bold**), the points are more important. However, a tiebreak, because it is occurs at the end of a set, *exhibits higher values of point importance than a standard game right at its inception and these values increase steadily to very high levels*. The first tiebreak point is worth more than three times the deuce point in the first game of the match (compare .226 with .062 –Table 3).

Because point importance values are more than doubling from the start of the tiebreak to the end, it means that a player who determines that she needs to play aggressively is far better off attempting this near the start of the breaker rather than near the finish. Again, this is the simple principle that riskier plays are more likely to succeed when there is less pressure. Less pressure makes it more likely that a player will attain her optimal arousal level and thus a higher probability of executing her play.

How often have you seen a player play conservatively, i.e., scared, at the start of the tiebreak only to take a wild cut at the ball at 4-6? This is precisely the wrong way to play a tiebreak as shown by the "Importance of the Point" values.

The relative point importance values strongly suggest a higher level of risk for the receiver when playing the first point of the tiebreak. If the server should miss his first serve and the second serve is average or weak, the returner should go for an aggressive return. Less importance means a better chance to make the return. With a 1-0 lead and 2 points as a server to follow, this is a perfect time to take control of the tiebreak.

Once you have seized the lead in a tiebreak, gear selection becomes paramount. When your opponent is down by a mini-break, you should be asking: which gear, steady (3rd) or aggressive (4th) gives me the best chance to win one of the two points when my opponent is serving? This is the basic Steady/Aggressive lens which we have discussed.

For example, let's say that the decision is to be Aggressive against a very average serve and you, the returner, miss the first return. Here is where you must trust your ability to execute and remain in 4th gear for the next point. This remains your best choice for winning one of the two points! However, after an error, many players scale back and this plays right into the hands of the opponent who is attempting to come back.

Here's an example of using point importance to analyze the Cincinnati final 2012: Roger Federer vs. Novak Djokovic. Result: Federer d. Djokovic 6-0, 7-6 (7).

After a lackluster start, Djokovic steadied his game to force a 2nd set tiebreak. Since their career record on outdoor hard court was 8-8 at this point, the 50/50 paradigm is perfect for analyzing the tiebreak. Federer won the first point against the

Djokovic serve by taking risk and he controlled the point. He then followed it up by winning both points on his serve, one with a service winner, to take a 3-0 lead. Given that Djokovic is known for his extremely consistent play when under pressure, Federer made the appropriate choice on the next point by intentionally hitting a short backhand return of serve to immediately pull Djokovic up to the net and out of his comfort zone. The return was just wide, however, and Federer now led by 3-1. It was at this point that Federer made a nearly fatal decision in terms of risk. As explained above, a player should "bundle" an opponent's serves into either a "Steady" or "Aggressive" pair. This is because the operative question with a 3-0 lead is: which type of point (Steady or Aggressive) should be played in order to maximize my chance of winning one of the two points? Federer played the 3-1 point very conservatively electing to slice the ball in play. Djokovic controlled him and forced an error on the 4th ball. This not only gave Djokovic the point, but it allowed him to regain some confidence by hitting several good shots back-to-back. Ultimately, Federer won the tiebreak by 9-7. Yes, Federer won the tiebreak and the match. But he nearly gave the breaker away at 3-1 when he played much too conservatively!

Players of all levels need to be more aware of risk management in the tiebreak and the implications of "bundling" their risk when the opponent is serving. This means choosing either 3rd gear (Steady) or 4th gear (Aggressive) on both points!

Set Probabilities with Unequal Opponents

All of the examples above used exactly equal (50-50) players as the basis for comparison. The first thing to notice is that, for a tennis match to be close, the difference between opponents must be very, very close. I mentioned the 55/45 probability above (91% probability that the better player will win a match). A 60-40 split results in a match that the higher-level player wins 99.6% of the time. But, what if the difference between opponents is only marginal?

Imagine a match where you now hold a 52-48 advantage in the probability of winning points against your opponent. The most immediate fact which stands out is that a 2% change in points won results in a predicted probability of winning 64% of sets played as well as over 70% of matches played! No other statistic better supports the claim which I made in the Introduction: I can make you a much better tennis player, and I need to only make you 2% better to achieve this!

Table 5

Probability of 52% player winning the set with tiebreak

ser \ rec	0	1	2	3	4	5	6
0	**.640**	.512	.369	.227	.107	.029	0
1	.745	.629	.486	.325	.170	.053	0
2	.839	.747	.617	.452	.265	.097	0
3	.915	.853	.753	.604	.404	.176	0
4	.966	.934	.875	.769	.590	.319	0
5	.992	.983	.962	.915	.811	.581	.310
6	1	1	1	1	1	.803	**.563**
						1	

Table 5 shows the probabilities that you will win a set in a 52-48 matchup. At the start of the match, this probability is 64%. However, your probability of winning a tiebreak is only 56.3%. This is simply because a tiebreak involves fewer points than a full set – thus there is more of a chance that luck will determine the outcome. It is crucial that you understand why there is a better chance to win at the start of the set as opposed to the tiebreak. If you are the better player, the more points that are played, the more chance there is that the "cream will rise to the top", i.e., that you will win.

Set importance when better player wins/losses first set

What does set importance have to say about your chances of winning when you lose the first set? What does it say if you should win the first set?

Table 6

Probability of winning match with 52/48 advantage

Match	0	1	2
0	.705	.539	0
1	.870	.705	0
2	1	1	

Table 6 tells a very important story. With a 52/48 advantage, the better player who loses the first set still has nearly a 54% probability of winning the match (the cell highlighted in red)! And, if he can tie the score at 1-set all, he once again becomes the favorite 70.5% of the time. Essentially, this means that better players can afford to WAIT for their opportunities. If you are the better player, there is no need to rush your comeback. Just keep playing – it will happen. And what will usually happen is the story told by Table 7.

Table 7 answers the question: what happens to pressure when you win or lose the first set if you are the favorite? If you win the first set, the importance of the second set declines slightly from .33 to .29. This allows you to relax and take a few more risks. If you should lose the first set however, the importance of the second set becomes extraordinarily large (again, notice the value of the red cell). This is where I would expect the stress levels of the match to cause your opponent (the underdog) to underperform. The weaker player must be a first-rate match manager in order to pull off the upset.

Table 7 – Importance of the set in a 52/48 match

Imp set	0	1
0	.332	.705
1	.295	1

This notion of WAITING (popularized by WAIT by Frank Partnoy) and, to my mind, often implemented by Roger Federer, is the implementation of patience applied to the score. Nearly all competitive players, particularly those who excel on clay courts, know the value of patience within a point. Going for too big a shot too soon will result in too many unforced errors. Similarly, even when they are playing fairly well, many players change their games when they fall behind in the score. I would suggest that you try to WAIT: keep playing the same and allow the score pressure to lower the performance level of your opponent. I believe that if you WAIT, opportunities to get back into the thick of the match will almost always present themselves.

For example, I was in a practice doubles match against two of the better 4.0 men at the club recently. They were playing extremely well and they went up by 5-3 serving for the set. I reminded myself to WAIT. A couple of double faults and then a couple of good returns later, we had broken and went on to win the tiebreak 7-0. The second set was a 6-1 bashing. WAIT!

Point importance at high levels of play

At the top levels of tennis, players are rarely winning only 50% of the points when they are serving. Usually, the percentage of points won on serve can reach around 60% except when the top players in the world are involved. They are all excellent defenders, so the actual numbers are somewhat below 60% when they play against one another. Let's look at the importance numbers for the 2012 US Open Men's final of 2012: Novak Djokovic versus Andy Murray.

Before exploring the details of this epic match, it is important for you to recognize that, once serving is a significant advantage, break point (30-40) is the most important point in each of the scoring snapshots below. The break points are all highlighted in red. This means that the "Importance of the Point" framework supports the conventional wisdom that break points are the most important.

It would be possible to calculate the point values for each and every point in the match (a long and tedious process – this would be the equivalent of a moving picture). But the concept which I hope you will grasp is easily illustrated by providing a scoring snapshot (like a single photo) at several key moments in the match: Table 8. After a slow start, Djokovic came back to tie the first set at 5-all. Notice that the point values at this moment are higher than any others except for the final panel (the fifth set). At this moment in the match, Djokovic faltered slightly and lost the first set 7-6.

To start the second set, Djokovic had sort of a meltdown and quickly went down 0-4. At this moment (the second panel), the points are worth 5-6 times less than at the end of the first set. He then staged a monumental comeback, playing brilliantly, to reach 5-all. Djokovic played his best when it was not very important only to falter and lose the second set 7-5. At this moment those who believe in momentum would be strongly favoring Murray to win. (I believe in "Point Importance" – can you tell?)

At the start of both the 3rd and 4th sets, the point importance values are still below those at the end of the 1st set. Once again, with relatively little pressure, Djokovic raised his game and he was able to tie the match at 2 sets all. Again, momentum points in the wrong direction – it suggests a Djokovic victory given that he had just won sets 3 and 4.

In the fifth and deciding set, the point values naturally reach their highest values. It was at this moment in the match that Djokovic once again faltered with a low first-serve percentage and numerous unforced errors. Taken as a whole, this suggests that Murray's ability to handle pressure was the difference in the match.

Admittedly, other explanations are possible. The wind was extremely difficult that day and Djokovic could also have tired in the 5th. However, my own assessment is that his between-point management routines let him down. These management routines are crucial at all levels of tennis and you should all recognize that learning the 4-D System will make each of you much tougher to beat because your between-point routines will have significantly improved.

Djokovic is not alone in his inability to handle pressure (at least in this one match). Paserman's research paper shows that female professional tennis players have this same weakness as a group. Using point importance data from Grand Slams in 2006, he shows that 33% of points end with unforced errors when the points are in the least stressful quartile (25%) of the point importance distribution. But the percentage of points ending with an unforced error rises to nearly 41% when the points are in the top quartile of the importance distribution. Even pros need to do better with their ability to handle pressure.

This panel of point importance at snapshots during the Djokovic/Murray match also serves to illustrate another key piece of information:

THERE ARE RELATIVELY FEW POINTS IN A TENNIS MATCH THAT HAVE THE POTENTIAL TO CHANGE THE OUTCOME.

Once you realize this as a player, it should help you to relax much more during the 90% of the time that point importance is relatively low. Relaxing will help you to perform better. But remember, relaxing does not mean not giving your best effort; it simply means playing from a calmer place.

Table 8

US Open — **Importance of point in match**

5-all 1st set

ser\rec	0	15	30	40
0	.054	.064	.063	.039
15	.046	.066	.080	.068
30	.030	.055	.089	.119
40	.123	.029	.067	.089

0-4 2nd set

ser\rec	0	15	30	40
0	.009	.011	.011	.007
15	.008	.011	.014	.012
30	.005	.010	.016	.021
40	.002	.005	.012	.016

0-0 3rd set

ser\rec	0	15	30	40
0	.022	.027	.027	.016
15	.019	.027	.034	.029
30	.013	.023	.037	.050
40	.005	.012	.028	.037

0-0 4th set

ser\rec	0	15	30	40
0	.041	.049	.048	.030
15	.035	.050	.061	.052
30	.023	.042	.068	.091
40	.009	.022	.051	.068

0-0 5th set

ser\rec	0	15	30	40
0	.075	.089	.087	.054
15	.063	.091	.112	.095
30	.042	.076	.124	.166
40	.017	.040	.093	.124

Setting the Table

There is another way to look at the scoring system of tennis: the score within a game is path dependent. This means that once the first point has been played and the score is either 15-0 or 0-15, one half of the outcomes as to how the game will unfold are eliminated.

In professional baseball, if the first batter in an inning gets on base, (this is called "Setting the Table"), his probability of scoring is around 37%. It is substantially lower if he gets on base with either one or two outs. Similarly, if the first pitch to any batter is a strike, the MLB (Major League Baseball) batting average is .227. If the first pitch is a ball, the average hitter now hits .278. The first pitch may make a hitter either mediocre or slightly above average.

In tennis, in a 50/50 match, the winner of the first point has a 65.6% chance of winning the game. The probability of winning the game increases to 81% once the score is 30-0, and 94% if the score should go to 40-0! Getting the lead within a game also means that point importance has dropped. This is an alternative way of demonstrating how a player can use the score as a way to build confidence. See the following example:

In 1989, I played a quarterfinal in a local tournament against the #4 player in the country in the M35s. He was a better player than I, but I noticed the first time that I played and lost to him in three sets earlier in the year, that he was prone to being overconfident. In the quarterfinal, I lost the first set 6-4, but I had played very well, so I decided to keep playing the same and hope that things would turn around. After winning the 2nd set, I started to use the "Setting the Table" concept in the following way: As I said above, this opponent was prone to overconfidence. This manifested itself with him playing high-risk tennis on the first two points each and every time that I served. I countered this by playing "solid" tennis on the first two points – high % of ¾-speed first serves, deep 3rd-gear groundstrokes, etc. At 30-0, he would then

back off a gear. This is when I was able to go on the attack, knowing that I'd get a ball which I could go after. Game, set, match Schewior! ☺

Summary

All points in tennis are not worth the same. This is obvious to any casual observer. However, the ability to use the score to inform yourself as to when more risk should be taken will make you a far better match player. Understanding the score and incorporating this understanding into your game plan and shot selection by adjusting the gear at which you play at any given moment of a match is a crucial element in improving your game. Here is yet another example from professional tennis:

At the year-end Championships in London in 2011, Roger Federer met David Ferrer. At 5-all 15-40 in the first set, Ferrer missed his first serve. Point importance considerations should have Federer attempting to be extra aggressive at this moment. He was. He hit a high pace forehand right down the middle, but missed the shot by a couple of inches. Nevertheless, he went on to break and win the first set 7-5. In the first game of the second set, Ferrer again went down 15-40 and second serve. Federer again was very aggressive, but this time he hit his forehand right in the corner for a winner! The point importance at this moment was low and Federer took advantage of this by choosing a riskier target.

I reviewed the risk implications of the lop-sided score (40-0 or 0-40) within a game with a former world-class player, Australian Open doubles semifinalist John James, and asked if he agreed. He replied: "It depends" and he went on to say that 40-0 in the first game of a match is a lot different than 40-0 at 4-5. Compare Table 3 with Table 9 below. It turns out that the values of point importance support his position. The value of getting the 40-0 point at 4-5 (.031) is more than twice that of the first game of the match (.015). His intuition and the point importance values agree.

Table 9

four-five	0	15	30	40
0	.078	.078	.063	.031
15	.078	.094	.094	.063
30	.063	.094	.125	.125
40	.031	.063	.125	.125

Chapter 8

How to Begin a Match: Build a Fire

Match preparation begins with your pre-match routine. The modern routine involves dynamic stretching before stepping out on the court (see the USTA website for details). For me, a short ride on a stationary bike followed by static stretching/relaxation exercises help most to bring me to the place where I'm ready to FEEL the ball once I step out onto the court. You should each develop and use a pre-match routine as much as possible when preparing for play.

The warmup should immediately follow the pre-match routine. For me, the ideal is to have completed the warmup at least an hour before the start of my match. This way there is an easy transition to being ready to play right at the start of the match. However, circumstances do not always allow for anything but a 5- to 10-minute warmup. You should occasionally practice getting right into a practice set with only a short warmup so that you are better acquainted with how you should acclimate to this shorter warmup.

All tennis players begin a match with some nerves. This is because of the uncertainty of playing against a new opponent or, even if you've played and beaten someone before, the uncertainty of whether or not your opponent played near her best level the last time that you met. Typically, two or three games must go by before you feel like you can play your game.

The metaphor which I like for beginning a match is "Build a Fire." If you are impatient when building a fire and you try to light the big logs first without adequately getting the kindling well lit and hot, your fire will go out. On the other hand, if you light the kindling well, but fail to add the big logs, your fire will also go out. In some matches (when you are the better player), you may rely on a smaller fire, but even in this case you should be aware of "Building a Fire" because you will need this skill against opponents of equal or higher ability in a later round or later in your competitive season.

It is important to understand that your opponent is experiencing the same set of nerves as you are! This means that you do NOT need to come out of the gate playing your best tennis. You only need to play good tennis for the first few games. Concretely this should manifest itself in the following ways:

Get a high percentage of first serves in to your opponent's weaker side. Solid ¾ speed first serves should work. There is no need to start the match with full speed first serves. Frequently, serving at full speed at the start of the match results in too many faults, and also, because you are nervous, several double faults. Confidence in your serve will erode. This is not the solid foundation upon which you would want to construct the remainder of the match.

When you are receiving, hit all of your returns deep down the middle and focus on seeing the blur. This gives your opponent no angles to work with and you get to establish your ability to see the "after image." If you should get a lead and your opponent is giving you many second serves, take a chance with an aggressive return. If you make it, you've already begun to rattle him; if you miss, you've taken an important step towards getting over your nerves and being able to play as you want to for the remainder of the match.

Play solidly and consistently from the baseline adhering to the principles of percentage tennis. Notice the situations in which your opponent chooses to violate the maxims of percentage tennis. These will come in handy later in the match when it is time to close him out. Most players hit their favorite shots at the start of a match. They want to feel comfortable on the court. Every shot that your opponent hits tells you something about her! As you become more adept at processing this information, your ability to find the appropriate tactics against each and

every opponent will improve so that small adjustments can be made earlier in a match rather than waiting until the end of the first set.

Creating Freedom

Every competitive player knows the feeling when he's hitting freely and with confidence. For some, this happens only in practice. For others, it's here one day, then gone the next. The purpose of this section is to talk a bit about how to create this freedom for yourself so that you are more able to access your "true game." Creating Freedom must be balanced with Building a Fire. These two ideas work hand-in-hand to get you into a match firing on all cylinders.

Matches are nearly always played with higher levels of stress than practice and this can translate into playing more tentatively. Each of the concrete steps below will inch you towards your free space. If done together, they virtually guarantee your freedom.

They include:

1) You need some relaxed non-competitive hitting where you are letting your racquet do the work in an effortless way. Remember, relaxed does not mean unfocused. Seeing each shot into the racquet is a must. This gets you in touch with playing the ball and NOT playing the opponent.
2) You should play some practice sets with people less skilled than you. There is no better way to feel your power! If you have a match against weaker opponents do not coast to victory. Instead you should be looking to hit freely on your way to victory. This will only help you for the future.
3) Each of you understands the cooperative nature of the warmup. However, in the warmup, you should access your freedom gear as well. There is no advantage to "hiding" this from your opponents. For example, when I warmup my opponent's volleys, I place the ball in 2nd or 3rd gear right to them for 5, 6, or 7 in a row ... and then I take the next ball and rifle it down the alley at Mach 100. I am beginning to create my

freedom and I send them a costless message: here is what you can expect once the match starts!

4) I make certain that somewhere within the first game I hit the ball exactly as I want to. This does not mean killing the ball – it does mean hitting freely. This goal is MORE IMPORTANT than winning the point. Here is the tradeoff: I am trading the possibility of losing one point at the start of the match (when points are not worth very much) for my ability to play freely for the rest of the match. Obviously, this is an easy decision. You can think of this as making a down payment for future success. Paul Annacone, former coach of Roger Federer and Tennis Channel commentator, speaks frequently of "investing" in certain plays or patterns early in a match.

For example, "investing" in a play might mean driving down the alley early in a match against an aggressive net player in doubles. Or it might mean attacking an opponent's second serve early in a match in singles. In both cases, the opponent is made to fear your choices.

Creating Freedom is a similar idea. Sometimes, it's important to invest in your freedom well into a match.

In a recent 8.0 mixed match a 6-3, 3-0 lead became 6-3, 4-3 as the balls became darker and darker on an indoor Har-tru court. We were the more aggressive team but were beginning to "Hold on for Dear Life." After bringing the game to deuce several times (but without freedom), I decided to invest in my freedom with an aggressive forehand return. I missed it long, but I got my freedom back. An easy love hold with aggressive play led to the 6-3, 7-6 win!

How to Finish a Match - Using the 4-D System to Avoid Choking

All tennis players have choked at one time or another, so it is interesting to see what the 4-D System would say about it. Choking is characterized by playing "tight" or "scared." Usually this happens when a player finds himself in winning position, but is having difficulty in closing the match. This means that the player is focusing excessively on the finish line or the "Importance of the Point" and is not making the transition into 3 and 4 (Calming Down and Ball Watching). Choking can be overcome by simply sticking to the 4-D structure. It is almost as if you no longer have time to "choke" because the process of digesting and then preparing for the next point takes up all of the time between points.

> ***Maria Sharapova is a wonderful example of this. Her between-point rituals take up all of the time between points leaving her with little or no opportunity to get nervous.***

Choking can manifest itself in either of two ways when looked at in the context of the 4-D System. First, as noted above, excessive body tension may throw off a player's FEEL. Either a player will overhit from trying too hard on important points or will slow down the gear of previously successful plays so that they are no longer effective. Alternatively, a player will skip through the Adjust/Plan step (2) when under pressure and make poor decisions when it comes to shot selection.

> ***For example, a player who has successfully pushed his opponent with well- placed and -paced groundstrokes suddenly uses a drop shot near the end of a set. The opponent runs it down and hits it for a winner. If you can maintain the 4-D sequence of steps, this will dramatically lower the probability of choking.***

Or, a player may fail to adjust the risk level based upon the score.

Just the other day, as an underdog pair, I was receiving serve at 3-all, 0-40 in a close doubles match. I failed to play in the correct gear – I was too cautious. They came back to win the set 6-3.

Chapter 9

Framing Your Expectations

Other Factors Affecting the Start of a Match:

Expectations

"The expectations of life depend upon diligence; the mechanic that would perfect his work must first sharpen his tools." Confucius

Most tennis matches begin with you in either the role of the favorite or that of the underdog. Only occasionally will both you and your opponent show up to play thinking that each of you will win the match – the neutral situation. Whether or not you have played one another before or not, i.e. have a match history, the role of the favorite is exactly the same as if you have previously defeated that player. And, the same is true if you should show up as the underdog. The toughest matches to play are the neutral matches where there is no strong inclination to favor either you or your opponent.

All matches should begin with a healthy respect for one's opponent. Essentially, this means that you are saying something like: "She is good and I am good. This is going to be an excellent match." Sometimes, when you are the underdog, it happens that you will give too much respect to the opponent.

For example, I poach in doubles against an excellent returner who hits behind me down the line, but misses the shot by an inch. Too much respect would have me reacting with "he had me. I had better not poach anymore." Healthy respect would have me react as follows: "he read that play, but he missed it. I need to try this again and see if I can get him really rattled."

It is also common that players will over-hit when they are the underdogs, thinking that they must "play great" or they will certainly lose. While it may be true that more risk must be taken occasionally to defeat a quality opponent, it is far more true that "playing great" is most often all about gear management. If you play high percentage tennis and play at the edge of your gears, you will have a chance to pull off the upset. Do not succumb to the trap of over-hitting against better opponents.

Conversely, it can happen that when you are the favorite, you go in with a complacent attitude. In situations like this, you need to remind yourself of the reasons why you are the favorite. It is usually because you have a way of exposing this particular player's weaknesses. If you play too conservatively and just keep the ball in play, this advantage disappears and you will be in a struggle.

Healthy respect for an opponent immediately translates into implementing the pre-match preparations which you have developed for yourself. When you are in your pre-match preparation, you should also review your game plan. Particularly when you are the favorite, it is easy to rush through both your preparation and your planning. Respect for your opponent demands that you stick with the regimen that you have developed whether or not you are the favorite, the underdog, or up against an evenly-matched opponent.

To sum it up: YOUR EXPECTATIONS SHOULD BE THAT YOU WILL STICK TO YOUR GAME PLAN AND NEVER GET DISCOURAGED NO MATTER WHAT THE SCORE. Expectations regarding the result (winning vs. losing) will only keep you from focusing on the right things during the course of a match. So, it should look like this:

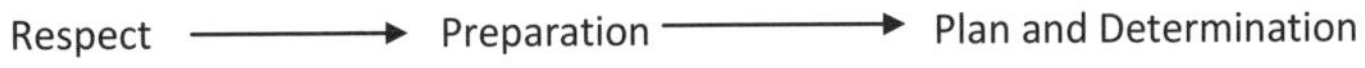

Expectations: Trial Runs

Whether it is individual competition, where the draws have come out, or a team competition, where you have a really good idea as to whom you will play against, there is a lot of time to over-think things in the few days before a match. Players will typically go through a series of trial runs before a big match, most of which are counter-productive. These counter-productive exercises almost always involve "tests" which you will either pass or fail. You will most often fail because the mental processes of the "test" differ from those which you've been practicing.

In practice, a few days before a big match, I give myself the following instruction: "Go for your big forehand cross- court. You need this shot to win the match and you NEVER miss this shot, so let's just test to make sure that it's there." Guess what? I MISS THE SHOT!

These "tests" are counter-productive because they erode confidence. This habit of being too judgmental is typical of the buildup to big matches for many players. By the time that they arrive to play the actual match, they have succeeded in knocking their confidence down a level or two. Now, there is almost no chance that they will play near their capabilities.

As you have seen in Chapter 3, confidence is actually something that can be "manufactured." By the same token, it is also something that can be eroded through poor pre-match framing and processes.

As I noted above, almost all players are nervous, to some degree, at the start of a match. This is normal and usually beneficial, i.e., it is a signal to yourself that you care about the outcome. However, there is a large difference between nerves and "worrying." "Worrying" forms a negative feedback loop which only serves to undermine confidence. The best technique for minimizing worry is immediately to redirect your attention to a picture of yourself executing a particular shot precisely as you would like to. In this way the negative "worrying" loop is broken and the energy of "worrying" is transformed into a positive confidence-building experience, the experience being the visualization of success.

An alternative way of viewing the "worry" dynamic is to notice that worrying involves thoughts. Worriers typically barrage themselves with a series of questions and doubts that run on and on. Visualization, however, is the polar opposite of the worrying process. A picture is substituted for the barrage of thoughts. And a picture, as the saying goes, "is worth a thousand words."

Recently, a strong 4.5 singles player experienced a slump following a vacation. Time away from the game had taken the edge off of her play. She asked me what she could do. "Linger at contact with your eyes," I said. "See yourself making ideal contact." She immediately changed the subject to a list of problems: "I'm pushing my backhand, my serve is off (but I can fix that on my own – don't know why I mentioned it), I'm missing the shots which I can always rely upon, I don't know if I should be coming to the net more …." She obviously needs to find a way to get to a quieter place and the way is through visualization.

Another top player at my club responds to my compliments in our practices as she approaches a big match with comments like "yeah, but I can't do it on my backhand" or "I'm just not handling the deep balls well" – this after pushing me to the back fence with consistent heavy depth. Make no mistake about it, these remarks can erode confidence as surely as a strong opponent can.

How to Frame a Match

Prospect theory, a recent development in economics, informs us that how we frame our choices has a significant effect on our decision-making.

In particular, prospect theory illustrates the built-in bias to play it safe. At the same time it suggests that the way out of this conundrum is to always take a big picture perspective. In general, the findings of prospect theory that are important for you as tennis players are three-fold:

1) The pain incurred from a loss is more significant than the joy derived from a win. Certainly, the realization that unforced errors explain the outcomes of nearly all matches also serves to make losses more painful.

This effect suggests that you will play too cautiously in some situations because of the "fear of losing."

2) Framing each match as part of a larger picture – not just an individual win or loss – but as part of an entire season of wins and losses will reduce the amount of pressure which you put on yourself for any one match. This, in turn, should allow you to play more freely throughout an entire season.

Framing any match within the context of an entire season is very similar to what professional stock traders do. If they were to evaluate each single trade as a gain or loss, they would tend to be too risk averse. Professional traders know that losses are part of making money and studies have shown that when amateurs are instructed to "trade like a professional," their risk-taking and overall returns go up. To complete the stock trading analogy: focusing excessively on any one gain (win) or loss can be paralyzing. By contrast, when a professional looks at any individual stock trade within the context of his overall wealth, it provides him with a much more stable basis for making decisions, i.e., setting an appropriate level of risk-taking.

Similarly, professional tennis players know that anything can happen on a given day and they are simultaneously evaluating any individual match performance and also looking at the big picture.

3) In experiments with identical rewards/losses, the choices that people make are a function of the "reference point," i.e., the starting point, before the game is played. When the payoffs are framed in terms of gains, players are more risk averse; when they are framed in terms of losses, they are more likely to choose a riskier option.

In the second round of Wimbledon 2012, Lukas Rosol chose and stuck with the riskier option in his upset of Rafael Nadal. In the deciding 5th set he hit 20 winners and only 2 unforced errors!

This has important implications for the favorite/underdog paradigm that I discussed above. Many tennis players, even when they know that they are the underdog, set the reference point at zero. In fact, they should be setting the reference point at some loss value because, unless something extraordinary happens, they will lose. They need to embrace the riskier option (playing with more courage).

> ***2nd seeded Simona Halep was beaten by the qualifier Zhang Shuai in the first round of the 2016 Australian Open. Halep remarked after the match: "I think it wasn't my good day but I give her a lot of credit as she played without fear and hit every ball." In other words, Zhang Shuai chose the correct reference point – if she had played with her usual amount of risk, she most likely would have lost.***

Prospect theory also points out the difference between episodic and thematic framing. With episodic framing, each match, game, point, is an event unto itself. There is no connection to a larger context. With thematic framing, on the other hand, you are always checking in with the big picture. Tactically within a match this means checking back in with your game plan even when you've just lost the previous point. And, in your post-match evaluation, you should be looking at your development over the course of a full season or even longer -- a college career, for example.

THE BOTTOM LINE: IF YOU PLAY TO NEVER LOSE, YOU GUARANTEE THAT YOU WILL CERTAINLY LOSE.

The Audience Problem

Family, friends, coaches, teammates, countrymen, parents, opponents, and opponents' support teams – each of these has an influence on the way in which you see yourself as a player. Expectations regarding your potential performance are present from each of these sources and each *may* influence your ability to be able to FEEL your shots.

Sam Stosur, who has elevated her game to the point where she is a legitimate contender in Grand Slams, has had very limited success in her home country of Australia. I had a similar problem at one stage of my own career. I did not play nearly as well in singles in New Jersey where I grew up. I was a far better player in my new home, Westchester County, New York.

As tennis players and people, our expectations and self-images are potentially a reflection of both our own perceptions and the perceptions of others. To the extent that the perceptions of others make us deviate from our own self-image, we undermine the confidence which comes from our own solid knowledge of who we are. There was a period in my late 20s when I choked a few matches in a row. Word quickly got out that I had difficulty finishing matches. I worked on it and got over it by using the tools that I am showing you.

When the perceptions of others intrude too much, it is absolutely essential to retreat to the practice court. Practice, in this case, becomes a kind of safe haven within which our tennis identities can be worked out and/or discovered.

In my opinion, players who think that simply playing more matches will make them into better players are missing a key link in the process of improvement. Your ideal should be to know your own game well enough so that only the most severe stress can derail you – we are, after all, human. Demanding complete perfection in this area, as in all others, will only lead to frustration.

In addition to visualization, this type of audience problem is best solved (can you guess by now?) by having solid between-point rituals which both insulate you from outside influences and bring you to a comfortable place where you feel at home. The sequence of these rituals is the heart of this book and it's the core of the 4-D System!

There is another related Audience Problem of playing in front of a hostile crowd. The solution again is the same. If you stay emotionally balanced and regain your composure between each and every point, you will be much more successful competing in these situations.

Match History

The start of a match where there is a history of winning and/or losing is particularly important and somewhat of a special case. Either both of you will be saying "it's business as usual" or "it's a brand new ballgame." It's important here once again to place expectations in their proper place. Your expectations should be to FEEL your shots and execute your game plan. Looking ahead to the result with thoughts like "I beat her last time; I have to win this time" are counter-productive.

If you have played someone before, your history is potentially able to have an effect on your expectations when you step out onto the court. If you won the first time, you have the benefit of knowing how you beat your opponent. You should immediately try to impose the same game plan and tactics so that your opponent gets the feeling "oh, no – here we go again." At the same time, you cannot take this opponent lightly as she is most likely looking to get some kind of revenge for the last time when she was beaten.

If you lost to your opponent the last time you played, you MUST be able to complete the following sentence in a positive way: "If I execute my plan to ..., I have a decent chance to win this match." This places the emphasis on the process of FEELING your shots and not the outcome of the match. As you have seen, this is key when attempting to get the most out of your game.

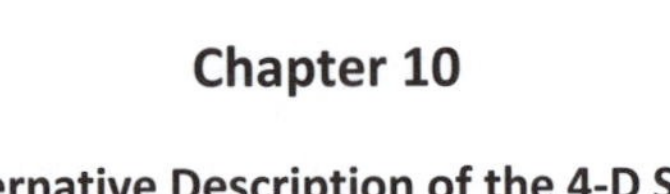

Chapter 10

n Alternative Description of the 4-D System

The four steps of the 4-D System may alternatively be thought of as requiring you to use four different types of attention between points. This supplemental description may help some of you to better grasp the conceptual structure of 4-D tennis and the mental dexterity that it requires.

A player's focus or attention can be described as varying along two dimensions: direction and width. First, focus is directional; it is either external or internal. External focus refers to a player's ability to pay attention to the world around him. Internal focus refers to a player's ability to be in touch with his thoughts and emotions.

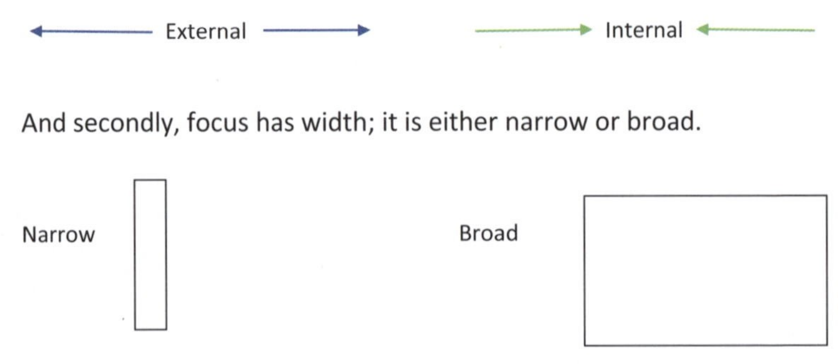

And secondly, focus has width; it is either narrow or broad.

An example of narrow focus would be watching the ball, while a broad focus might help a player to "see" which patterns of play are working to his advantage or disadvantage.

In the Attentional Direction diagram below, the sequence between points should always be ordered exactly as I said above: FOCUS SHOULD ALWAYS BEGIN IN QUADRANT 1 AND MOVE CLOCKWISE THROUGH EACH OF THE QUADRANTS, ENDING IN QUADRANT 4 JUST BEFORE AND WHILE THE BALL IS IN PLAY.

It is crucial for you to recognize that you can control
the width of your focus. And, it is equally critical that
quadrants I-IV be maintained. You can get into all sorts of trouble by changing the sequence or neglecting one of the steps.

For example, most players know that thinking about the previous point just as the next point is beginning is asking for trouble. This amounts to getting hung up in quadrant I without adequate preparation for starting the next point.

Attentional Direction

The 4-D System looks like this:

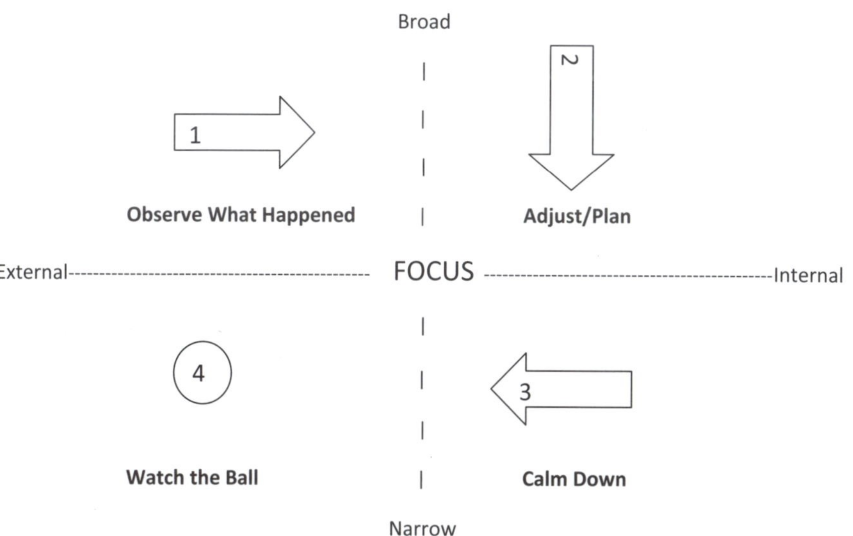

Narrow Internal Focus – Getting Stuck in Your Emotions

It is well known that when stress increases, people narrow their focus. Tennis is no exception. What this means is that players often respond to a tight situation by by-passing 1 and 2 and going to their feelings and staying in 3 (without calming down). This is the #1 trap of competitive tennis players – getting stuck in their negative emotions. Either of two things may happen as you become overloaded with self-doubt and criticism and fail to make the transition to Watch the Ball (4) that would allow you to execute effectively. First, as I just said, you could get stuck in 3 without ever calming down and never transition to 4. This is the most counter-productive reaction because no part of your mental game is functioning when you go to this place. Without the transition to 4, it is likely that the next point will be lost – and thus the downward spiral begins. Another error produces more stress which gets you further stuck in your head (negative feelings), leading to another missed transition into ball watching ... and so on.

Or, alternatively, you will calm down and transition to 4, but to the exclusion of being able to transition your focus to broad external (Observe What Happened) at the end of the point. This means that both of the broad focus or awareness components of a strong mental game become compromised. You are gradually losing your ability to "see" what is happening in the match. This might manifest itself by changing strategies or patterns of play either too frequently or not at all, with no hook on what is actually happening on the court. You may become so focused on your feelings and watching the ball that you are unable to make the appropriate tactical adjustments.

By learning to immediately redirect your attention at the conclusion of a point to "see" what happened, you will immediately bypass the possibility of getting caught up in negative emotions. This process is very similar to that of cognitive psychologists who teach their patients to substitute "correct" thoughts in place of the "wrong" thoughts that occasionally pop into their heads. The 4-D System helps enormously because it gets you immediately out of your own head and into the world around you.

Loser's Road Map: Avoid at all costs

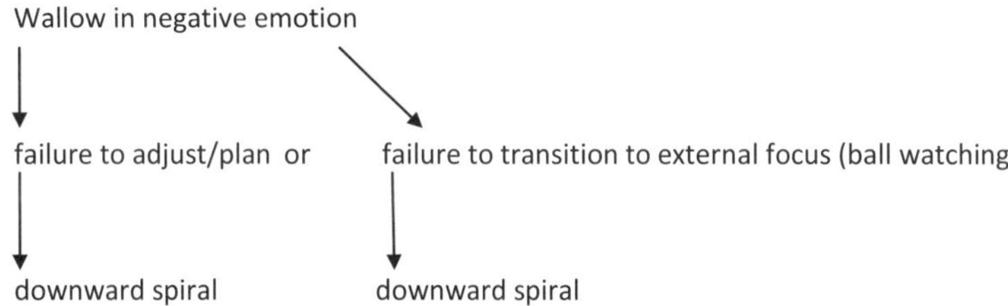

The implementation of the 4-D System takes practice and discipline. To my mind, it should be integrated into your game just as you would add a new stroke – play against weaker competition first to establish your new habits and discipline. Then gradually begin to ratchet up the level of competition and test your ability to stay within the system.

You will improve significantly if you adopt the 4-D System. But you would be wrong to think that it is easy. Like anything else that is worthwhile doing, it takes practice and effort to develop the 4-step process of the System. About how long might you expect it to take?

Maria Popova, chief author at the website *Brain Pickings*, provides us with an answer:

When he became interested in how long it takes for us to form or change a habit, psychologist Jeremy Dean found himself bombarded with the same magic answer from popular psychology websites and advice columns: 21 days. And yet, strangely — or perhaps predictably, for the internet — this one-size-fits-all number was being applied to everything from starting a running regimen to keeping a diary, but wasn't backed by any concrete data. In ***Making Habits, Breaking Habits: Why We Do Things, Why We Don't, and How to Make Any Change Stick*** — which also gave us this fascinating read on the psychology of self-control — Dean, whose training is in research, explores the existing empirical evidence on habit-formation. He cites one influential study that gives a more concrete answer to the elusive question of how long it takes for a new habit to take root:

The simple answer is that, on average, across the participants who provided enough data, it took 66 days until a habit was formed. As you might imagine, there was considerable variation in how long habits took to form depending on what people tried to do. People who resolved to drink a glass of water after breakfast were up to maximum automaticity after about 20 days, while those trying to eat a piece of fruit with lunch took at least twice as long to turn it into a habit. The exercise habit proved most tricky with "50 sit-ups after morning coffee," still not a habit after 84 days for one participant. "Walking for 10 minutes after breakfast," though, was turned into a habit after 50 days for another participant. [17]

What's more, when researchers plotted the results, they found a curved relationship between habit and automaticity — meaning that earlier repetitions were most beneficial for establishing a habit, and gains gradually dwindled over time. If you decide to add 4-D tennis to your game, then do it relentlessly ... and it should be yours within three months.

4-D can also be extended to more than just the time between points, although that is its key focus. In order to win a match against a difficult opponent, you must also be able to make constructive use of the changeovers.

Mental processes on changeovers

Players often do not make good use of the time on the changeovers. Besides hydrating and resting (sitting down), a player should remind herself of what she is doing right if she is ahead in the score. This requires a check in with Adjust/Plan (2) during the changeover. Frequently, players squander a lead because they are not adequately in touch with what they are doing correctly. Maintaining contact with what's working will help you to focus and plan for the game at hand, as well as to have tools prepared to deal with a comeback attempt by the opponent.

For example, if I am serving to my opponent's backhand and getting control of nearly every point, and then I mysteriously stop using that target, I need to be able to get to my winning

[17] "How Long It Takes To Form a New Habit", by Maria Popova, Jan. 2, 2014. From the website: Brain Pickings.

tactic. I must understand how I built my lead so that I can go back to my winning pattern of play.

It is also important to consider that two games will be played before the next changeover. In the same way that football requires both an offense and a defense and different tactics for each, so does tennis require a different game plan depending upon whether or not a player is serving or receiving. The first game to be played following the changeover should receive the lion's share of attention, but the following game should not be ignored. For example, a player might be receiving first and remind herself to use the (up until this moment) successful lob over the netman as a way to get control of the net, but also visualize, however briefly, how poaching against the forehand of the deuce-court returner has been a winning pattern for her team. In effect then, the changeover becomes a time where a player checks in with her game plan and then visualizes winning BOTH games.

Changeovers also occur at the end of a set and should be used to make adjustments to a player's overall game plan. The decision at this time either to change or not to change her overall plan should be based upon the same sort of judgment that was used to determine which patterns of play should be REPEATED and/or AVOIDED.

Let's look at the following two scenarios: First, a player has just lost the set 6-4. She held six break points at one time or another during the set, but played too tentatively to capitalize. In her last service game, she double-faulted twice to lose her serve. She lost the game because her nerves got the better of her. Similarly, nervous play contributed to her inability to break serve. This player should NOT change her game plan. But she would need to recognize that she needs to do a better job of calming herself down between points and staying in the correct gear – connecting better with quadrants 2 and 3.

To take another example, suppose that a doubles team has just lost a set 6-4. They have managed to hold serve each time except for once, but have failed to get more than one point in any game when the opposition is serving. They are starting each receiving point in the standard hot-seat formation, i.e. the receiver's partner at the service line. It is now definitely time to play both back and attempt to lengthen the points. There is compelling evidence at this moment that the first game plan will not work and it should be changed. Remember, changing a game plan never comes with a guarantee of success. The only thing that it guarantees is that you will not keep on losing the same way for the entire match!

In doubles, there is an additional component whenever you are in step 1. While observing what just happened on the court, you should also check in on your partner. Depending upon the personality of your partner, a comment may or may not be warranted (some players prefer more talking; others prefer less). However, a positive "yeah!" is always a good idea after a particularly good play from your partner. On the changeovers, this contact should be more detailed, reviewing what is going well, etc. And it should also include a personal component which entails the ability to say things that will help your partner to focus and relax.

Tactical changes are nearly always reserved for the changeovers. Players who change their tactics in response to each and every point essentially do not have a strategy. They are simply blowing with the wind. This reveals a most basic misunderstanding of having a good game plan – it is not to win each and every point, but rather to win more than the opponents do by the time you shake hands. In doubles, partners who talk "too much" about what they are "seeing" usually are not seeing anything.

Post-match Analysis – A Key to Further Improvement

A match, particularly a close one which hinged on just a few points, is a fantastic opportunity to see how your mental game is evolving. There are two basic ways of evaluating your ability to implement the 4-D System: 1) did you rush through or simply forget to visit any of the four steps between each and every point? and; 2) did you get "stuck" in any of the four steps to the detriment of ignoring some/all of the others?

Rushing through the steps of 4-D is very common when you first begin to implement the system. As I said above, excessive pressure will cause you to narrow your focus too much. Making use of practice matches to get comfortable with the 4-D structure is very important. In addition, the more you try it out, the easier it will become for you to stick to the program. Like any other part of tennis, practice will make you more perfect.

If you are the type of player who gets "stuck" without transitioning to the entire 4-step sequence, you are going to have to devote a lot of concentration to eliminate this way of going. The most egregious offenders are those players who cannot overcome their negative emotions in step 3. You must put your focus on displaying zero negative emotions in practice so that you know what it's like for a match.

> ***Players who bellow or exclaim loudly after each missed shot are not even close to using the 4-D System. If you play a player like this, it should give you confidence because you have a skill which they don't possess.***

Post-match analysis naturally involves more than just your ability to implement the 4-D system. You may have technical or endurance issues which prevent you from going to the next level. This is not within the scope of this book, but I would remind you that all technical practice must be done with FEEL. This means that repetition alone will not make you a better player; only mindful repetition will do this.

Personal Attentional Styles

Most players have a preferred attentional style. For example, if you have a well-developed external focus (1 and 2) you will be able to "see" what an opponent is doing and come up with possible solutions to solving the strategic puzzle. However, you may not be able successfully to transition to steps 3 and 4 and may lack the internal focus necessary to execute your plan. If you fit this description, you must play a substantial number of practice sets wherein you are required to notify your coach before each point that you have transitioned to an internal focus before the start of each point.

One useful signal that a player has transitioned to an internal focus is "eye flashing." Serena Williams uses this technique. As a returner of serve, Serena's eyes "flash in" to a small area surrounding herself and then back out again to the server. Her eyes flash until just before the server begins her motion at which time she looks out to see the ball leave her opponent's strings. This keeps her focused on her #1 task at this moment – see the ball into the strings – as well as makes it more possible for her eyes to (literally) have the ball in better focus at contact.

Other players are well locked-in to the ball, but lack the external focus needed to "see" what is happening on the court. If this is your issue, you should repeatedly play live-ball drills that emphasize the various responses to differing situations. Over time, you will come to know the "Percentage Tennis" response to nearly every situation. Your coach should gradually increase the complexity of the decision-making until you can instantaneously recognize and adjust to what you are "seeing." The concept of "The Snapshot" discussed earlier should be used in practice until it becomes a habit.

Summary

The 4-D System allows a player to be engaged with all of the components of a complete mental game. If you learn to play within this system, you will see immediate rewards as well as largely eliminating choking as a problem.

At this time, it's helpful to review what getting stuck in the various quadrants means. To the extent that you can identify yourself as more likely to break down in a certain mental place in the sequence, you will become all the more able to come up with a fix.

Step I fixation: These are the players who dwell way too long on what just happened on the previous point. They make few or random adjustments and are unprepared for the start of the next point.

Step II fixation: Here are the players who think that there is always a magic tactical bullet in each and every match. They spend so much time varying their games and looking for a weakness that they have no central game plan guiding their play. Frequently, they are not good ball watchers.

Step III fixation: This is perhaps the most common group. These players have an inability to let go of emotional attachment to their errors. They are the players most easily caught up in a downward spiral.

Step IV fixation: Players in this group have excellent ball watching skills, but they are completely oblivious to what's happening tactically on the court. Many times their shot selection is purely random, rather than being driven by the matchup of their opponent's strengths and weaknesses with their own.

Chapter 11

Momentum and the 4-D System

Does momentum exist in tennis? This is an extremely important question for us to answer within the framework of the 4-D System. If it exists, then we would hope that the 4-D System would allow us to manage it better. If it doesn't exist, then it can be ignored and you can play comfortably within the System.

The use of the word momentum suggests that what has just happened will continue to have an effect on the immediate future. Similar to the "hot hand" framework in basketball which holds that Player A is more likely to hit the game-winning shot if he is "hot," i.e., has made a high percentage of his recent shots, momentum in tennis might mean: if I've just won a point, does it increase the likelihood that I will win the next point? It could also ask: if I've just won a game, does that increase the likelihood of winning the next game? The same question could also be asked at the level of the set because of the unique scoring system of tennis.

If the answer is yes, then the 4-D System is built to limit the momentum of your opponent, while at the same time propelling your own. This is because 4-D allows a player to "recover" between each point. This recovery will mute the effects of an opponent's strong play (because you will make adjustments) and propel your own strong play forward by maintaining touch with your game plan and your focus.

Momentum can be real or it can be psychological. Either way, 4-D takes care of it. One formal test is a point-by-point analysis using sophisticated statistical tools to answer the question: does winning (losing) a point on serve make it more (less) likely that I will win the next point on serve? The results from professional tennis suggest that there is momentum, but that it is not of a very large magnitude when compared to point importance. Once the quality differences between players are accounted for, Klaassen and Magnus report that there is a .9% increase for men and a 1.2% increase for women in the likelihood of winning point on serve if you have won the previous point on serve. Klaassen and

Magnus also report on the effects of the relative frequency of the previous ten service points won on the likelihood of winning a point on serve. There is no effect. Together, these results strongly suggest that "the recent past" has no meaningful effect on the present. This contrasts with anecdotal reporting of momentum by sports broadcasters in tennis and many other sports.

An Example of Point Momentum

Momentum advocates would have you understand the implications of the score by saying that there are psychological or other effects which result from the path which leads to any given score. For example, here are two entirely different ways of getting to deuce:

Path 1:

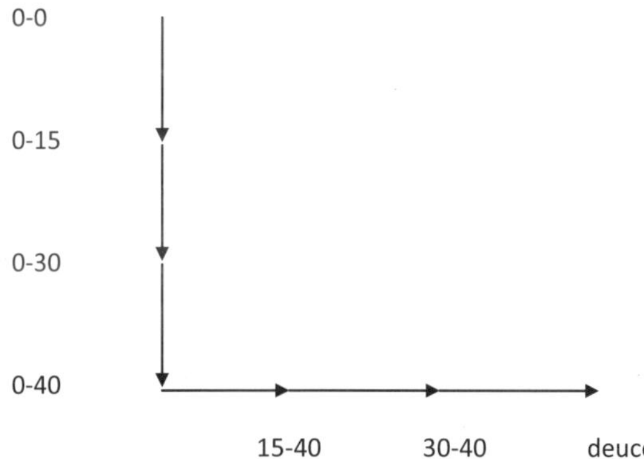

In other words, following Path #1, the server goes down 0-40 only to fight his way back to deuce. Now, a momentum advocate would claim that the returner had momentum at 0-40, but then "lost his momentum" or "the momentum switched." Remember, if momentum means anything, it means that the immediate past will carry weight into the future. Clearly, it doesn't exist for the returner and it remains to be seen if it exists for the server. (How many times have you heard tennis commentators saying that he "lost his momentum"? This is simply hogwash!) Certainly, since serving is an advantage, we would expect the server to win more of the games from deuce.

Path 2:

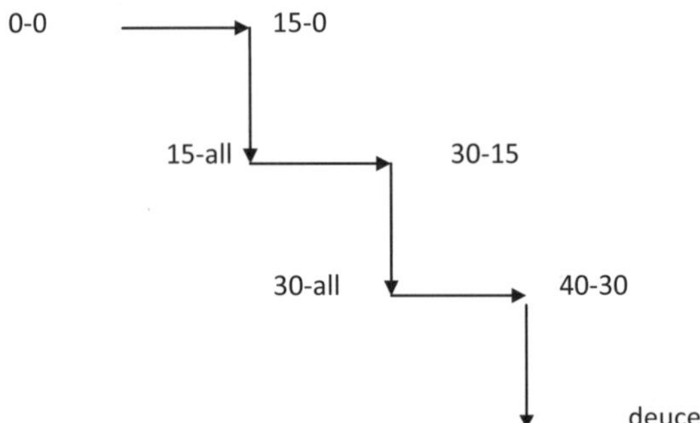

Following Path #2, the server and receiver alternate points until deuce is reached. There is no momentum being generated by either player. Once again, arriving at deuce, we would have to give an edge to the server as serving is an advantage. What counts at deuce is the score and the score alone! The path to getting there is irrelevant.

Economists talk about this as two different ways of understanding any given phenomenon: 1) Path dependence – this is the explanation of momentum advocates – the way that you get there matters; or 2) State dependence – this is the claim of point importance advocates (me!). State dependence means that only the score matters and NOT how you got there.

Recall the evidence from top-level professional players: momentum does not exist for the top players. My explanation is that they are using the 4-D System or something very similar. Players with a strong mental game eradicate the emotional ups and downs of a match and play to the score without regard for the path which got them to the place where they are.

BE HERE NOW!

So, I ask again, does momentum exist in tennis? The answer depends crucially upon the definition of momentum which we choose to use. It is important to distinguish between momentum from point to point and momentum given a certain game score. Anecdotal reporting of momentum by sports broadcasters in tennis is usually made with respect to the game score.

For example, many tennis broadcasters typically use momentum as a substitute for "player X is in the lead." If I am ahead by 4-1 in the 2nd set after losing the first, does this mean that I have "momentum"? If we go back and look at our 50/50 match, having momentum in this case simply means that the player in the lead will most likely win. Imagine a coin tossing game where one of the outcomes (heads) leads by 7-4 with the first to 10 being the winner. Heads will win most of the contests simply because he has the lead – it has nothing to do with momentum. It does not suggest anything about any possible effect of this lead upon future points yet to be played. This rather nonsensical use of the word momentum is best captured when sportscasters use expressions like: "he had the momentum only five minutes ago and now the momentum has shifted totally in the opposite direction," i.e., the lead has disappeared.

In a first round match at the Monte Carlo Masters in 2014, Edouard Roger-Vasselin led Pablo Andujar by a set and a break. He was broken back only to find himself with 3 break points when Andujar served at 5-all, 0-40. Certainly, at this moment (as well as when he had the set and break lead), R-V had the "momentum." Andujar went on to win nine straight points to level the match at 1 set all. Certainly, at this moment, Andujar had the "momentum." He was immediately broken and the momentum went back to R-V who was also broken! They then traded breaks in the next two games as well suggesting two more "momentum shifts." Andujar went on to win the match 7-6(5) in the 3rd. The story of the match was not "momentum," but rather the simple fact that R-V could not see himself as the winner of the match.

Chuck Kriese, the longtime great and successful men's tennis coach at Clemson, has a momentum management system in his book, Total Tennis Training. Kreise would argue that the score is not that important – what matters far more is the flow of the match and how you and your opponent arrived at a certain moment in the match. Significantly, he calls for playing for the forced error when you are ahead by one point in the game echoing a key concept from Chapter 6. However, he also calls for playing a long point at 40-0 or 0-40 – a direct contradiction of a key finding in Chapter 5. I would suggest that all of you watch professional tennis to see which type of point predominates at these extremes in the score. The pros are pros for a reason – they (mostly) understand how to play based upon the score.

Kriese also suggests playing with the following characteristics when you are behind in the score: 1) Play within your limitations; 2) Avoid unforced errors; 3) Become more aggressive. Typically #2 and #3 are mutually exclusive, i.e., I cannot simultaneously make fewer unforced errors while becoming more aggressive. In fact, his formula directly contradicts the Steady-Aggressive framework that we developed in Chapter 3. (If any of you knows how to do this, please let me know!). Kriese then goes on to tell the story of one of his players who was down by 6-3, 4-1 in doubles and then played "reckless" tennis and came back to win. He never addresses the question: how does reckless tennis fit with "playing within your limitations"? In fact, he seems to be suggesting, using the things that you have learned up until this point in the book, that taking more risk when the points are relatively unimportant (you are almost certainly going to lose at 6-3, 4-1 down) is the correct way to go – and to hell with the limitations! After all, it's just a game – better to go out in flames than with a whimper.

In addition, Kriese suggests running your "bread and butter" play when the score is tied. I would completely agree based upon the Importance of the Point discussion in Chapter 5. You should be running your best Percentage Tennis plays when the score is close, reserving your other plays for the (relatively) unimportant points. In the end, Kriese doesn't say much that I would disagree with. However, I would frame the discussion differently. Rather than classifying playing modes as either "Chain-Saw Killing" or "tentative," the issue can all be handled under the rubric of gear management. The "Chain Saw" being the situation where a player goes to 4th gear too soon in a point and the "tentative" case being the one where the player retreats to 2nd gear – what I have called

Holding on for Dear Life. Using 4-D to manage gears between points will take care of these issues.

Alistair Higham has written an entire book on momentum - Momentum: the Hidden Force in Tennis. He begins by defining momentum as "the force that controls the flow of a match." He goes on to add that "it is a hidden force" and that it is "invisible because it comes from the flow of energy between players." He then goes on to ask: "How is it that some players always manage to get momentum on their side when it matters most"?

My answer is that these players are simply better players and a part of being "better" is having something like the 4-D System or its close equivalent as a part of their arsenal. Later, when speaking about the "turning points" in a match, Higham goes on to say that there are not turning points, per se, but rather only *potential turning points*. He adds: "it's not what goes wrong that's important, but your response to what goes wrong." 4-D has a built-in self-correcting component. By refusing to go to the emotional center at the conclusion of a point and directing your focus to what just happened, 4-D effectively provides you with an effective counter to your opponent's momentum. (My point is that momentum does not exist if you are using the 4-D System.)

Many of Higham's other talking points are built into the 4-D System. For example, he emphasizes: 1) know how you got there; 2) understand the scoring system; 3) spot patterns of play; and 4) review your tactics.

THESE ARE ALL A PART OF 4-D. THE DIFFERENCE BETWEEN 4-D AND HIGHHAM'S MOMENTUM APPROACH IS THAT THE 4-D SYSTEM IS SYSTEMATIC -- IT IS USED AFTER EACH POINT.

Let's continue to look at the game score within a set. Certainly, it seems plausible that a first set tied at 4-all is quite different depending upon the path which the score took to get there. Imagine scenario #1 where you and your opponent have held serve to 4-all and scenario #2 where you raced to a 4-0 lead and your opponent has come back to tie the score. Higham's analysis would suggest that there is no momentum is scenario #1 while there was a gargantuan momentum shift under scenario #2 – first, it was completely in your favor; now, it is completely against you. (Here is where I have real trouble seeing momentum when you are ahead by 4-0. If momentum exists, then a 4-0 lead should translate into a 6-0 or 6-1 set. Since it did not, there was no momentum at that stage of the match – there was only a 4-0 lead!).

An Example of Game Momentum

Game momentum tells the same story: the order in which games are won or lost is irrelevant to what will happen next.

For example, Scenario #2 from the above paragraph:

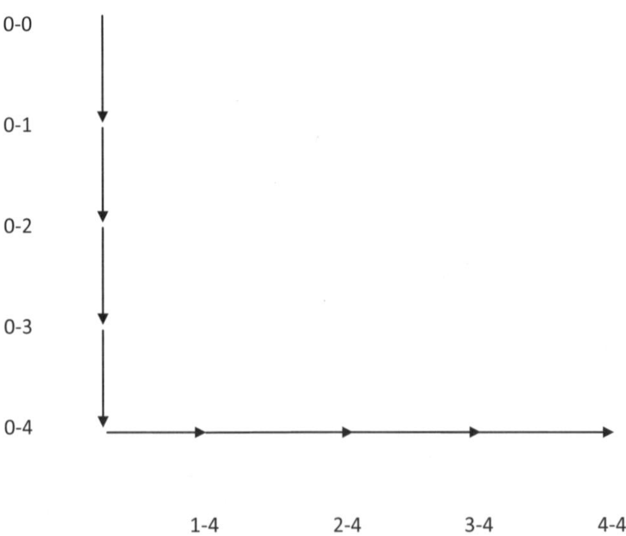

In other words, following Scenario #2, the server goes down 0-4 only to fight his way back to 4-all. Now, a momentum advocate would claim that the returner had momentum at 0-4, but then "lost his momentum" or "the momentum switched." Remember, if momentum means anything, it means that the immediate past will carry weight into the future. Clearly, it doesn't exist for the returner who squandered a 4-0 lead. At 4-all, we might be tempted to say that the server, who has now won 4 straight games, has the momentum. But, we might then ask: if there was no meaning in the term for the receiver, why should there be any meaning now? The Djokovic-Murray US Open final which I described in detail in Chapter 7 makes this all vividly clear.

About the only thing that that we can say with full confidence at 4-all is that we are getting near the end of the set and, therefore, the points are becoming more important.

No matter the path to the 4-all score, the 4-D System would have you ready and focused to play at this moment in the match. Yes, scenario #2 suggests that you have to make some adjustments at this point, but that's just a part of having a solid mental game.

MOMENTUM IS MEANINGLESS WHEN YOU IMPLEMENT THE 4-D SYSTEM.

How about momentum across sets? In an article published in *Tennis Week* (July 2006), I wrote the following:

So, given that it's difficult (if not impossible) to analyze momentum at the micro level of "within the game," I propose to analyze momentum at the macro level of the match. The starting point is to recognize that two players are precisely equal at two points during a match. The first is trivial. It is right at the start of the match. The second is much more interesting. It occurs when the players split sets in a 2-out-of-3 set match. *However, not only are the players tied, but one of them, the one who won the 2nd set, has momentum.*

The testable hypothesis here is: does momentum matter when players are evenly matched, i.e., tied after two sets? The answer to this question also implies certain conclusions. For example, if momentum is found to matter, then this suggests that either the winning player is "learning" as the match progresses or the emotional balance has tipped in his favor. Conversely, if it turns out that momentum has no effect on the outcome of matches, then this would suggest that the scoring sequence has no impact on the outcome. Both players would focus and perform equally well during the third set. This would mean that the third set would literally be like the toss of a fair coin, i.e., a 50-50 chance for both players.

The data used to investigate the momentum hypothesis is from the 2005 Men's Professional Tour. All of the data were gathered from Stevegtennis, a popular website with the results of all of the professional tournaments. All tournaments in 2005 are included in the data with the exception of the Grand Slams which play a 3/5 format. As mentioned above, the number of first- and second-set winners will be compared to the expected results from the repeated toss of a fair coin. Using the binomial theorem, I calculate the probability that a fair coin would produce the observed result. A high probability suggests that the coin is not fair, i.e., that momentum exists.

The results are reported in Table 10 below. There were 741 3-set matches on the Men's Tour in 2005. Of these, 386 (52.1%) were won by the player who won the 2nd set, and 355 were won by the player who won the first set. The prob-value that this percentage of 2nd set winners would be greater than the observed number (386) strictly by chance is .135. While this probability is quite low, it falls just outside of the standard confidence interval most widely used in the social sciences to analyze statistical significance (.1). I conclude that, while the data are suggestive of a small momentum effect (2.1%), I cannot reject the hypothesis that these results were generated by the repeated toss of a fair coin.

Table 10

Sample	# of matches	first	second	% first	% second	prob
Full	741	355	386	47.9%	52.1%	0.135
Grass	61	41	20	67.2%	32.8%	0.998
Hard	372	177	195	47.6%	52.4%	0.189
Clay	261	114	147	43.7%	56.3%	0.024
Carpet	47	23	24	48.9%	51.1%	0.500
Outdoor	565	272	293	48.1%	51.9%	0.200
Indoor	166	77	89	46.4%	53.6%	0.198

When broken down further by court surface, the momentum hypothesis seems to hold only on clay. Without getting into an involved discussion, my guess is that this is the result of "learning." There is less room for luck on clay once an opponent "figures you out" because the points last longer.

If you think about it a bit more, then the test that I conducted above to detect momentum suffers from a potential defect: two players are not really equal at the start of a match. One player is always ranked higher than the other. I adjust the momentum data with the following rules: 1) if a seeded player plays against an unseeded player, he is "seeded"; 2) if a higher seed plays a lower seed, he is "seeded"; 3) if two unseeded players play each other, they can be regarded as "equals."

When the data is adjusted to take account of 3-set matches between "equals," the results are truly astounding. Of the 288 3-set matches between equals, the first set winner wins 143 matches (49.7%) and the second set winner 145 matches (50.3%). Momentum is clearly a chimera with the exception of matches played on clay. On clay, 2nd-set winners win 57% of all 3-set matches between "equals."

So, momentum can really only be said to exist on clay, where 56-57% of the 3rd set winners exhibit momentum depending on the model used to estimate momentum. Yet, this effect is still fairly small (6-7%). As suggested above, the absence of momentum could mean a high level of competency in dealing with adversity. If this is true then perhaps results from junior tennis, where a player's mental skills are not as well developed as those of the pros, would show that momentum does, in fact, exist. To investigate this, I looked at all main draw matches from L1+ B14 Eastern tournaments from 2005 (L1+ are the top-level sectional events. Most participants go on to play college tennis.) Of the 106 3-set matches played, 55, or 51.9%, were won by the player who won the second set.

Momentum doesn't explain much when it's stripped down to its essentials. The fact that the player with momentum wins about 52% of the time is not very different from a coin flip. The small difference declines to zero when I account for the relative quality of players in a match. The fact that momentum is often confused with the fact that the team (or player) with the lead tends to win, or the team that scores more than the opposition ends up victorious, is circular thinking at its worst.

So, all things considered, momentum is nearly as uneventful as the Unremarkable Hypothesis (teams in the lead tend to win) and its Corollary (score more than they do and you will win). Therefore, if momentum is not a meaningful lens through which to understand tennis matches, the natural question is: is there a better lens? Yes. As we saw in Chapter 5, Point Importance provides a far better foundation for understanding what is happening in a tennis match.

I implore each of you to understand the implications of this discussion:

1) 4-D, because it requires that you touch base with what you are doing right, provides you with an excellent framework for maintaining the pressure on an opponent.
2) 4-D, because it requires that you change/adjust your tactics when confronted with falling behind, provides you with an excellent tool for halting your opponent's good run of play.

Let's look at the Djokovic-Murray US Open final of 2012. This is the match where I provided several point importance snapshots at key moments of the match. Certainly, when Murray led 7-6, 4-0 he had the momentum, but Djokovic came back to tie the score at 5-all before dropping the 2nd set 7-5. Surely now Murray had the momentum leading by 2-0 in sets. Again, Djokovic came back to tie the match at 2 sets all. Here the momentum proponents would say that Djokovic now had the momentum, but now Murray came back to win the 5th set by 6-4.

My own opinion is that players like Murray and Djokovic, who have extremely high competence in their between-point rituals, are not subject to negative momentum. No matter the score, both of these players are always looking to adjust and find a way to win. I also believe that, if both of these players are playing at their peaks, Djokovic is the better player because he is more capable of playing offense. This suggests that his flaw in this match was not being in close enough touch with what he was doing right. When it got to closing time at the end of the first, second, and fifth sets, he was uncertain of how to play. Particularly in the fifth set he seemed to under-appreciate how important his first serve would be in looking to control the match.

Chapter 12

Summing It Up

Now that the game has been deconstructed, it is time for you to put the pieces together in a way that is both intelligent and suits your personality.

My own prejudices with respect to my tennis amount to two:

1) I believe in the power of the mind and I believe that the mind can achieve amazing things – especially when it knows how and when to get out of the way of the body. Train your mind and you will see how well you can play. There is no better feeling than accessing the space where you can just let it go when it counts!
2) I love playing offense! Certainly, as in chess, a solid defense is necessary (the 3rd gear foundation), but the joy and the fun comes from a potent offense and the creativity which having an all-court game permits.

In the Introduction, I mentioned that a mere 2% improvement in your tennis game can have a large impact on the outcome of a match. If you perfect the 4-D System, you can improve by 2% in *each* of the four areas of the System. In other words, your improvement will most likely be far more significant than I promised you when you began this book.

Step #1 of the System requires you to stay in touch with what just happened on the court. In doing so, your ability to make the adjustments necessary for victory is enhanced. As I said above, players sometimes lose touch with what they are doing right. Often a comeback from opponents is due more to a letup by the player in the lead rather than a tactical adjustment by the trailing player. Learning how to "play the same" is an invaluable skill.

Step #2 corrects shot selection errors both with respect to the targets and the gear levels which are chosen. Certainly playing Percentage Tennis will make you a far more intelligent player.

Step #3 will improve your execution as well as making your risk-taking rational rather than haphazard. There is statistical proof from professional tennis that improving your performance on important points can raise your game by 2%.

And finally, in Step #4, your ability to implement better "gaze control" will reduce unforced errors and improve your ability to hit your targets.

Many of the top players in the world play at a very deliberate pace. This is certainly because they are employing some version of the 4-D System. Now you can do the same.

In the end, the 4-D System offers you the following: Approach your tennis game with discipline and you will begin to play with more intelligence, more freedom, more trust, and more courage ... it doesn't get much better than that!

Bibliography

Bhalla, Happy http://zennistennis.com/Articles/The trap of the big point theory

Fox, Allen Tennis: Winning the Mental Match Kearney NE: Morris Publishing, 2010.

Gallwey, Tim The Inner Game of Tennis New York: Random House, 1974.

Gonzalez-Diaz, Julio, Gossner, Oliver, and Rogers, Brian W. "Performing Best When It Matters Most: Evidence From Professional Tennis", *Journal of Economic Behavior and Organization,* 2012, **84**, (3), p. 767-781.

Harbach, Chad, The Art of Fielding New York: Little Brown, 2011.

Higham, Alistair Momentum: The Hidden Force in Tennis Lansing, Michigan: Coachwise Ltd, 2000.

Klaassen, Franc J.G.M. and Magnus, Jan R. "Are Points in Tennis Independent and Identically Distributed? Evidence from a Dynamic Binary Panel Data Model", *Journal of the American Statistical Association*, 96(454), June 2001, pp. 500-509

Klaassen, Franc and Magnus, Jan R. Analyzing Wimbledon: The Power of Statistics New York: Oxford University Press, 2014.

Kriese, Chuck Total Tennis Training Indianapolis, IN: Masters Press, 1988.

Loehr, James PhD. The New Toughness Training for Sports New York: Penguin Group, 1994.

Partnoy, Frank WAIT: The Art and Science of Delay New York: Public Affairs, 2012.

Paserman M. Daniele, *Gender Differences in Performance in Competitive Environments? Evidence from Professional Tennis Players,* Boston University, January 2010, unpublished paper.

Reid, Machar, Elliott, Bruce and Crespo, Miguel Tennis Science: how player and racquet work together Chicago: U. of Chicago Press 2015.

Sun Tzu The Art of War New York: Writer's Club Press, 2002.

Walker, M. and Wooters, J. "Minimax Play at Wimbledon." *American Economic Review* 91 (5):1521-1538 Dec 2001.

Wallace, David Foster A Supposedly Fun Thing I'll Never Do Again "Tennis Player Michael Joyce's Professional Artistry as a Paradigm of Certain Stuff about Choice, Freedom, Discipline, Joy, Grotesquerie, and Human Completeness New York: Back Bay Books, 1998, p. 213-255.

Wiles, Joel "Mixed Strategy Equilibrium in Tennis Serves" Duke University Honors Thesis, April 2006.

About the Author

Robert W. (Bob) Schewior has been Director of Tennis at the Chestnut Ridge Racquet Club in Mt. Kisco, NY since 1976. He has coached numerous juniors to national rankings and his adult teams have often made it to playoffs in USTA leagues. He has been a certified USPTA Professional for over 25 years.

Bob played #1 singles for Rutgers University from 1971-73. In the late 1970's and early '80's, he was Westchester County Champion as well as Westchester County Indoor Champion several times. In 1980 he was the New Jersey State doubles champion. Bob reached his peak as a player between 1987 and 1990, when he was ranked in the Top 20 in both the 35- and 40-and-over National USTA rankings in both singles and doubles. At that time, injuries forced him to retire from more active competitive play.

Bob has had two articles published in Gene Scott's *Tennis Week*: Feel in Tennis, Feb. 7, 1980 and How to Watch a Match, July 2006.

In the early 1990's Bob returned to college where he earned his Ph.D. in Economics from Rutgers University. He has the unique ability to be able to use the insights of economics to explain many key elements of playing excellent tennis in a way that is new and refreshing.

Bob lives with his wife, Jane, in Katonah, NY. You may contact the author by visiting his website: DeconstructingTennis.com.

Acknowledgements

First, I would like to thank many of my students who were willing to surrender some of their preconceptions in order to improve. Their trust allowed me to see that the things which I talk about here really work in competitive tennis. In particular, the players in the women's singles group at Chestnut, from which I provide numerous examples in the book, have all been instrumental in helping me to fine-tune the 4-D System and other related topics. Good students ask questions and these questions, in turn, continually demanded that I expand and refine my teaching. These players also provided invaluable support at the editing phase with their insightful comments.

Others have also contributed enormously to the editing process, most notably my stepson Brian Gutherman and my student, Julie Leff. Thanks to Julie, I will never write a split infinitive again! In addition, my longtime student, Amy Kaufman, was instrumental in directing me to make this book as clear and simple as my on court lessons.

My fellow pros have also been of great help over the years. When I first became a teaching professional in 1976 at the start of the "tennis boom," many of us were learning and discovering together. In particular, Christopher Busa, my first teaching partner at Chestnut Ridge Racquet Club in Mt. Kisco NY, was always searching for the secrets which would unlock great tennis. Fellow teaching/playing partners including Peter Bromley, Jeffrey Aarts, Tom Carey, and other Westchester pros were also instrumental in my development as a both a coach and a player.

I first played tennis with my parents from whom I learned many valuable lessons. In particular, I learned sportsmanship from my mom, Eleanore, and hating to lose from my dad, William. Hence using the "W" in my author's title as a tribute to all of the times he hit with me after school as a kid.

Finally, I would like to thank my wife, Jane, for encouraging me to write about things I know about. The advice and the system offered in this book are unique and honed over many years of teaching and playing. She encouraged me to put it all in writing.